DATE DUE

PRINTED IN U.S.A.

LOUIS PHILIPPE AND
THE JULY MONARCHY

PAUL H. BEIK

Professor of History
Swarthmore College

AN ANVIL ORIGINAL

under the general editorship of

LOUIS L. SNYDER

D. VAN NOSTRAND COMPANY, INC.

PRINCETON, NEW JERSEY

TORONTO   LONDON

NEW YORK

To
W.H.B. and S.W.B.

D. VAN NOSTRAND COMPANY, INC.
120 Alexander St., Princeton, New Jersey (*Principal office*); 24 West 40 St., New York, N.Y.
D. VAN NOSTRAND COMPANY (Canada), LTD.
25 Hollinger Rd., Toronto 16, Canada
D. VAN NOSTRAND COMPANY, LTD.
358, Kensington High Street, London, W.14, England

COPYRIGHT, 1965, BY
PAUL H. BEIK
Published simultaneously in Canada by
D. VAN NOSTRAND COMPANY (Canada), LTD.

PREFACE

Much of the pleasure which accompanied this project resulted from the obligation to fit together materials of great variety, for while the available evidence concerning Louis Philippe is not as plentiful as one could wish, that about the July Monarchy is very plentiful indeed. To some extent the man has been sacrificed to the regime, and certain aspects of the regime have been given priority over others. In the text, an effort has been made to apportion space to all of the significant topics, but in the readings it has been necessary to choose one or two of many possible themes. The readings, therefore, are devoted mainly to materials that describe events or illustrate political and social attitudes. The readings have been concentrated within the period 1830-1848 and have been selected for the most part from sources not readily accessible to students. All but two of the documents have been translated from the French by my wife, Doris Beik; her contribution greatly advanced the project and improved its product.

PAUL H. BEIK

Swarthmore, Pennsylvania

TABLE OF CONTENTS

Part 1

LOUIS PHILIPPE AND
THE JULY MONARCHY

— 1 —

THE MAN AND THE REGIME

King Louis Philippe I. Even to the liveliest of imaginations it is a long journey from the 16-year-old boy of 1789, Louis Philippe, son of the Duke of Orleans, to the 57-year-old man who in 1830 became Louis Philippe I, King of the French. One of the disadvantages of rapid surveys of history is that there is no time to get used to the enormity of people's experiences. Try to conceive of what it meant to live through a decade of revolution, then through a decade and a half under Napoleon, then through another decade and a half while the old France and the new tried to coexist in the Restoration, and *then* face the possibilities opend by the July Revolution of 1830. True, a whole generation passed this way—Metternich, for example, was born in 1773, the same year as Louis Philippe. But it mattered greatly where one was placed during this time, and Louis Philippe always found himself exposed between distasteful alternatives: the revolution and the counterrevolution, Napoleonic France and potential invaders, the Restoration kings and a mutinous public opinion. In 1830 an opportunity opened before him and he made a choice—with what thoughts it is impossible to know, but one can review his experiences and the major probabilities which he confronted.

"King Louis Philippe I," the title adopted in 1830, made the bearer something less and something more than a new king in the old dynasty; he was a new dynasty; otherwise he would have been Philippe VII (Philippe VI having been King of France in the 14th century). The title "King of the French," rather than "King of France," was a gesture of deference to the people's will. This etiquette was the sign of a new age.

The July Monarchy. Of the many French regimes, the one from July, 1830, to February, 1848, is frequently called the July Monarchy, after its parent revolution. Although Louis Philippe tried to found a new dynasty, he proved to be the last French king. Nothing could be the same in France after the great revolution of 1789-1799, and certainly not for a monarch whose crown had been passed to him in a revolution, but in 1830 the shape of the future was indistinct. Was this to be the French 1688, as some had predicted, with Louis Philippe playing the role of William III? To be sure, France was not England, and this was a new century, bursting with conflicting programs and attitudes. Was 1830 perhaps a renewal of 1789? It has sometimes been said that the 1789 to 1815 cycle of constitutional monarchy, republic, and Bonapartist dictatorship was rerun at a different speed between 1815 and 1870. This last parallel is tempting, for it dramatizes the principal French political traditions.

The Restoration and July Monarchy, with their charters, moderate liberalism, limited suffrage, bicameral legislatures, and relatively strong kings are reminiscent of the hopes of the moderate Anglophiles in the early months of the great revolution. One could argue that the French society of Louis Philippe's time had not changed so rapidly that its political possibilities were altogether different from those of 1789. Nevertheless, society was changing; the old slogans still carried their magic, but were bound to be differently interpreted; and there were new slogans.

Whether Louis Philippe with better luck and more wisdom could have altered the rhythm of French political development is an inevitable question. The answer must be that he could have done so, but it is less easy to say within what limits, given the conditions of the times. Certainly his personality and career had an important influence in rooting certain major tendencies in French political life.

The House of Orleans. In our own time, the pretender to an improbable French throne is the great-great grandson of Louis Philippe, Henri, Count of Paris (b. 1908), a rich and public-spirited man with a large family and considerable charm and newsworthiness. The grandfather of the present pretender was the Duke of Chartres

(1840-1910), who had served France in the Franco-Prussian war of 1870-1871 under an assumed name. That Duke of Chartres had a more famous older brother, the Count of Paris (1838-1894), who just missed being crowned king, following the Franco-Prussian war. These brothers were the grandsons of Louis Philippe. Their father —Louis Philippe's oldest son—was killed in a tragic carriage accident in 1842.

This Orleanist branch of the Bourbons, of which King Louis Philippe was the most successful member, had a rather troubled history that dated back to an ancestor who was the younger brother of Louis XIV. Being the younger brother of the Sun King was not an easy role, and Philippe (1640-1701) played it clumsily. His son, also Philippe (1674-1723), was regent during the minority of Louis XV. He became noted for his dissolute life and for his effort to bring the aristocracy into government by means of councils. His descendants all suffered from the awkwardness that they were Orleanist cousins of the ruling kings, who were automatically suspected of coveting the throne. Persons disgruntled with the regime always gathered around them. These tendencies were particularly noticeable in the case of Louis Philippe Joseph (1747-1793), father of the future King Louis Philippe.

Louis Philippe Joseph became head of the Orleans family in 1785 upon the death of his father and took the customary title Duke of Orleans. At that time he was 38 years old, rather tall and well-built, with a reputation for intelligence, charm, and idleness. He had performed military service but had been denied a promotion which he coveted. Marie Antoinette was said to detest him and he her. Critics of the court in the 1780's encouraged him to lead the opposition. On one occasion, in 1787, he said publicly and in the king's presence that illegal procedures were being used to force the Parlement of Paris to register a financial measure. The king, Louis XVI, was stung into exclaiming, "Yes, it is legal, because I will it," thereby dramatizing the conflict between absolute monarchy and the parlement.

The Duke of Orleans, very rich in his own right, had married an equally wealthy heiress. Their four children were the Duke of Chartres—future King Louis Philippe, born in 1773—his two younger brothers, Montpensier and Beaujolais, and a sister, Adelaide. The family's Paris residence was to be famous in the revolution: it was the Palais Royal, a stone's throw from the king's own Tuileries palace. The Duke of Orleans had enclosed the palace gardens in a huge square of handsome apartments overlooking lawns and flowerbeds, with shops for rent on the ground floor, along an arcade. These improvements had made the whole neighborhood much more fashionable, with the result that the duke's properties were very lucrative. Because of his easy manners, ready charity, and apparent sympathy for political reform, the Duke of Orleans became the focus of plots and manipulations during the revolution, and let himself be carried along by events, and as we shall see, his family with him.

— 2 —

AN EXTRAORDINARY PREPARATION

Louis Philippe had an extraordinary preparation for kingship, unplanned and unforeseen. He started life near the steps of the throne. His father's position as a potential replacement for Louis XVI, and later his own position as a possible alternative to Louis XVIII and to Charles X, kept him in the political picture. From his childhood there was a possibility that those who influenced him might, improbable though it was, be playing a part in history.

Childhood. Born in 1773, the future King Louis Philippe at the age of eight came under the influence of a strong-minded, ambitious, and practical woman. She was Madame de Genlis, daughter of a provincial noble, authoress, and former mistress of the Duke of Orleans. To assure her future and satisfy a genuine interest, she had persuaded the pliant duke to make her governess of his children. With the aid of tutors she organized the lives of a little troupe consisting of Louis Philippe, his sister Adelaide, his two younger brothers, and several other children, including a pretty English child renamed Pamela (rumored to be her own daughter by the duke). These children were trained to run, swim, and carry heavy weights. The boys were taught fencing, but Mme. de Genlis did not approve of hunting, and Louis Philippe in later life was to amuse people by his accounts of the idiocies of the hunt. Through days lasting from six in the morning to ten at night, the children learned mathematics, sciences, practical trades, some history and literature, and many languages: German in the morning and at lunch, English in the afternoon and at dinner, Italian in the evening, and occasionally Spanish. Mme. de Genlis wanted them to be hardy and self-reliant. She did not encourage them to be imaginative.

Mme. de Genlis found Louis Philippe a large, serious-

12

minded, somewhat timid boy. Her spartan regime gave him physical toughness and taught him to work hard, meet people, and give orders when necessary. He was thoughtful, and she encouraged his tendency to reason. Louis Philippe remained conscientious and painstaking and prosaic.

The Great Revolution. While Louis Philippe was reaching adolescence, his father was allowing himself to be used in other people's plans. It would be unjust to make too facile an appraisal of the intentions of the Duke of Orleans in these years, but it is certain that he was weak and self-indulgent and that his name and money attracted adventurers. Orleans—he had inherited that title in 1785, at which time young Louis Philippe became Duke of Chartres—was part of the "aristocratic rebellion" which forced the calling of the Estates General for 1789. In the election campaign he was probably coached by the future deputies Sieyès and Mirabeau; in any case he was able to influence opinion, and was himself chosen a deputy. His liberal posture was conspicuous.

The son, Louis Philippe, celebrated his 16th birthday on October 6, 1789, in the midst of the "October days," an insurrection which brought the royal family and National Assembly from Versailles to Paris. In the early morning hours of October 6 a mob had broken into the palace at Versailles and very nearly ended the life of the queen. If loyal troops had not intervened at the last moment, Marie Antoinette and possibly the whole royal family might have been killed. After the event gossips said that the Duke of Orleans had initiated the affair with such an outcome and his own succession in mind. There is no evidence of such a plot, but because the Duke of Orleans stood to profit, the circumstances damaged his already tottering reputation. After the October days the king sent Orleans on a diplomatic mission to England, together with agents to keep an eye on him.

In the summer of 1790 Orleans returned to France without permission, and shortly thereafter his son Louis Philippe joined the Jacobin club. The boy's mother opposed the move, but his father and Mme. de Genlis approved. In 1790 the Jacobins were moderate constitutional monarchists. Their new member's journal of this era shows

him still devoted to Mme. de Genlis, and altogether a
serious-minded, good-hearted young man, perhaps inclined
to take himself too seriously. As a spectator, Louis Philippe
also attended sessions of the National Assembly, but he
was soon made a colonel of dragoons and was transferred
to barracks life at Vendôme, on the Loire southwest of
Paris. While the revolution was becoming more radical,
the young patriot, in the first glow of professional enthusiasm for the military craft, was able to mature in less
controversial surroundings.

At the end of 1791 Louis Philippe and his regiment
were ordered to Flanders. When war came in 1792, the
French at first suffered setbacks, but Louis Philippe kept
his head and rallied his troops. On the home front the
monarchy fell on August 10, 1792. Louis Philippe's father,
elected to the Convention, sat with the radical Mountain
deputies and took the name Philippe Égalité. The son,
Louis Philippe, already a general, was cited for bravery
for his part in the famous artillery duel at Valmy where
the Prussian advance was stopped. In the later battles of
Jemappes (November, 1792) and Neerwinden (March,
1793) he distinguished himself. He now called himself
General Égalité. He was 19.

In Paris there were rumors that the new revolutionary
hero Danton was in the pay of an Orleans faction. Danton
did indeed want to stabilize the revolution before it went
to further extremes, and since Louis XVI was now a
prisoner and in danger of being executed for treason,
Danton wanted to save the king so that peace with Europe
would be possible. Danton probably considered various
alternatives to Louis XVI, among them a return to constitutional monarchy under Orleans or his son. Louis Philippe
during a visit to Paris just after the proclamation of the
republic in September, 1792, was advised by Danton to
keep clear of politics and make a military record—advice
which implied a restoration. Another person who had his
eye on Louis Philippe was General Dumouriez, his com-
manding officer on the Belgian front, a royalist on the
lookout for a chance to turn against the Convention.

Louis Philippe was in Paris briefly on the eve of the
king's trial but left before the fatal vote. He urged his
father not to vote and not even to attend the sessions at

which the king their relative was to be judged. But Philippe Égalité let himself be taken to the Convention and there let himself be persuaded to vote for his cousin's execution for treason, and then, to complete the awful logic of his position, voted against a motion for suspension of the death sentence. Louis XVI went to the scaffold on January 21, 1793.

Henceforth the name of Orleans carried a blemish which was not to disappear with Philippe Égalité's own execution during the Reign of Terror, and was to handicap Louis Philippe for many decades. More immediately, the royalist General Dumouriez pinned his hopes on Louis Philippe, whose enthusiasm for the revolution was waning. Dumouriez in early 1793 made an armistice with the Austrians, hoping that they would permit him to march on Paris. The Convention became suspicious, and prepared to arrest him. The general appealed to his soldiers, but they refused to follow him. Dumouriez had no choice but to take refuge with the Austrians (April 5, 1793). Louis Philippe, who was implicated because he had known of Dumouriez's plans, accompanied him. He had already sent abroad his sister Adelaide and Mme. de Genlis, who had been living near Dumouriez's headquarters. His father, mother, and two brothers were arrested by the revolutionaries, as he would have been, but for his flight.

Exile. Just approaching his 20th birthday, Louis Philippe in exile was almost without funds but refused a commission in the Austrian army because he feared reprisals against his relatives in France. In the summer of 1793 he was too controversial a figure to be welcomed anywhere. His father's vote for the execution of Louis XVI had inspired horror, and it was not safe for the son to be known by his right name. Leaving Mme. de Genlis and his sister in the care of some nuns, he set out on a walking tour in Switzerland. When the cold weather came, a family friend arranged for him to become Monsieur Chabos, an instructor of languages and mathematics in a Swiss secondary school. It was there that he learned in November, 1793, of his father's execution. Louis Philippe was now Duke of Orleans. Since adolescence he had been on the fringe of his father's political maneuverings, which had finally ended in the ridiculous posture of Égalité and then in death. The mark left by this fiasco was ineradicable, but the son's patience and endurance were to re-establish the family fortunes and, 37 years later, enable him to make a political bid of his own.

Meanwhile as a young teacher he became involved in an affair with Marianne Banzori, a servant girl at the school, whose pregnancy was the prelude to his departure at the end of the year. There followed travels in Germany, Scandinavia, and America. Louis Philippe was in America from 1796 to 1799 as part of a bargain with the French Directory, which restored to his mother her property, but not her husband's, and freed her two younger sons on condition that the three remaining Orleans males start a new life in the new world. Good relations with the Directory lapsed, and when the young men heard that their mother was in Spain they went to Havana by way of New Orleans and tried to ship for Spain but were denied entry and even expelled from Cuba by the Spanish government. They reached England in January, 1800.

All this time Louis Philippe was not altogether a forgotten man. A minority among French *émigrés* and perhaps a majority within France would have accepted a constitutional monarchy on the English model as the best means of ending the revolution. Louis Philippe because of his past record and current views was remembered as a possible replacement for the intransigent Louis XVIII, pretender since the death in captivity of Louis XVI's son. Louis XVIII's stubbornness contributed to the failure of the moderates to stabilize the situation within France. Napoleon Bonaparte in 1799 seized the role of stabilizer, and Louis XVIII did not until 1814 get another chance to compromise with French realities.

Upon his return from America, Louis Philippe ended his isolation and tried to contribute to the solidarity of the Bourbon house in its adversity. Although in the earlier days of his exile he had disapproved of Louis XVIII's absolutist stand, he now made a statement of principles acceptable to the exiled king and began to send him analyses of the European diplomatic scene.

Louis Philippe's younger brothers died in 1807 and 1808. He himself was by then in his mid-thirties, fairly tall, growing a little heavy, dignified, thoughtful, well-informed, self-confident, full of anecdotes, and convincing in argument. He was collecting a pension from the British government, and was also trying to convince the Spanish Bourbon rulers of Sicily to give him their daughter's hand in marriage. The princess, Marie Amelia, saw all of Louis Philippe's good qualities, but her mother, who happened to be the sister of the late French queen, Marie Antoinette, was naturally reluctant to permit an alliance with the son of Philippe Égalité. Louis Philippe eventually proved to her that he was not subversive, and the marriage took place in November, 1809.

In 1810 Louis Philippe went to Spain with visions of serving the Bourbon cause by heading the Spanish resistance to Napoleon. His benefactors the British did not want him to meddle in Spain, however, and forced his withdrawal. Once again he had missed fighting against French troops.

In the remaining years before Napoleon's downfall, while the tension in Europe mounted and the great duel in Russia gave way to French retreat and European uprisings, Louis Philippe was on the sidelines. On the island of Sicily his family, destined to be large and close-knit, began to grow. Ferdinand Philippe was born in 1810, Louise in 1812, Marie Christine in 1813, and Louis Charles Philippe in 1814, the year of a change in the family's fortunes.

The Restoration. When Napoleon abdicated in April, 1814, and left for the island of Elba, Louis XVIII was recalled to the French throne, entering Paris on May 3. In June he "granted" a Charter, maintaining an appearance of absolute monarchy, but actually the Restoration was a compromise with the revolution as consolidated by Napoleon. Where Napoleon had sat, the king now presided, with the help of a Chamber of Peers (some hereditary, some appointed for life) and a Chamber of Deputies elected with a very high property qualification. These bodies represented only the rich and well-born, and did not control the ministers named by the king, but France had representative government again despite the king's use of the white flag of his ancestors and his pretense that the Charter was a gift which could be rescinded.

This dramatic turn of the wheel of fortune brought Louis

Philippe back from Sicily to look after his interests. He was, indeed, among those considered as a replacement for Napoleon, and the British helped him to travel to France, but the issue was settled before his arrival. Louis XVIII restored to Louis Philippe his rank of Lieutenant General and such Orleans properties as were identifiable in the tangle of Philippe Égalité's estate. Louis Philippe found the Palais Royal partly rented and partly used for storage. He cleared the place for his family's return, then made a swift visit to England to check on the family holdings there; what these amounted to is uncertain. By September, 1814, he had returned to Palermo and moved his whole family to Paris.

After the brief winter season of 1814-1815, Napoleon came back from Elba. In the early part of the crisis, Louis Philippe was sent to serve under the king's brother Artois at Lyon, but Napoleon's rapid advance from Grenoble forced them to retreat. Louis Philippe sent his family to England, but would not himself leave France until told to do so by the king. When Napoleon proved invincible, the departing Louis XVIII gave Louis Philippe very flexible orders which enabled him to join his family in England. Once again he did not have to spoil his record of never helping foreign armies fight against France. Louis XVIII, however, did not forgive him for crossing to England instead of following his king to Ghent. During the Hundred Days of Napoleon's comeback the Orleans family was again discussed as an alternative dynasty. The great powers did not take up this suggestion, but Louis XVIII was naturally suspicious of his cousin. After Napoleon's defeat Louis Philippe had to make a hasty trip to Paris and renew his protestations of loyalty before he was permitted to recover his property.

The king, Louis XVIII, was overweight and immobilized by a defect in his hip. He was a clever, caustic man, not much liked by his associates, but capable of making himself respected. The Second Restoration was made difficult by the intransigence of the most reactionary of the returned *émigrés,* the Ultras, and by a white terror. Louis XVIII had no love for the new France that had emerged from the revolutionary and Napoleonic years, but he knew that he had to learn to live with it. Until 1820 he was able to pursue a course between the Ultra Royalists, who were devoted to the ideal of a Catholic, monarchical, socially stratified France, and the Independents, who looked to one or another version of the revolutionary tradition—liberal, Bonapartist, or republican. People who supported the Charter and Louis XVIII's efforts to make it work as a practical compromise were called Constitutionals or Doctrinaires.

Louis Philippe remained a controversial figure during the Second Restoration. The king appointed him to the Chamber of Peers, but liberals tended to gather around him, and he himself, while maintaining formally proper behavior, associated with liberals and bourgeois. In part as a result of a speech in the Chamber of Peers opposing the prevalent spirit of reaction, Louis Philippe was forced to leave France again, in October, 1815, and for two years he remained with his family at Twickenham, the Orleans home in England. For a time they were spied on by agents of the French ambassador, but in 1817 they were allowed to return to Paris.

In February, 1820, the Duke of Berry, Louis XVIII's nephew, was stabbed to death by a fanatic. His death seemed to assure the end of the elder Bourbon line. Louis XVIII was 65 and childless. Artois, his brother, was 63, and had, in addition to the murdered Berry, one other son, the Duke of Angoulême, who at 45 had not produced an heir. Suddenly the Orleans, who were next in line, seemed very close to the throne. But in September, 1820, more than seven months after the assassination of her husband, the Duchess of Berry gave birth to a boy, the Duke of Bordeaux (in later life sometimes called Count of Chambord). The "child of the miracle" saved the prospects of the elder Bourbon line. The Orleans family may not have been overjoyed at this turn of events, but whatever their true feelings, people supposed that they were disappointed. Inevitably there were rumors questioning the child's legitimacy, and the gossips who had interpreted Berry's murder as an Orleanist plot were also capable of blaming Louis Philippe for these rumors.

Family Affairs. During the Restoration, Louis Philippe's principal occupation was not politics, but straightening out his father's affairs. Philippe Égalité had accumu-

lated so many creditors that in spite of his great wealth he
had been forced during the revolution to declare a kind
of bankruptcy, turning over his assets and liabilities to the
state for eventual examination and accounting. The king
gave Louis Philippe his father's records, and with the help
of many lawyers Louis Philippe put the Orleans properties
on a sound footing again. Although already very rich, he
shared in the controversial *milliard des émigrés* of 1825,
by which compensation was paid to former *émigrés* for
their losses during the revolution. Louis Philippe's mother,
who died in 1821, left an enormous fortune. The old
Prince of Condé, whose son the Duke of Enghien had
been executed in 1804 at Napoleon's orders, willed his
beautiful chateau and domain of Chantilly to Louis Philippe's son, the Duke of Aumale.

The Orleans family was growing. Without listing two
children who died in infancy, there were five boys and
three girls. They got along rather well with each other,
with their parents, and with their aunt Adelaide, who
shared her brother's common sense and political interests.
Louis Philippe presided over this family circle like any
bourgeois father, but he was also an 18th-century figure
who had know the court at Versailles, the revolutionary
clubs and army, and the *émigré* dispersion. He was something of a pedagogue, but his family listened with respect
to the tales of his extraordinary life.

Louis Philippe cherished the Orleans political potential
as carefully as any of the family holdings. He was a model
of propriety in his relations with the kings Louis XVIII
and (from 1824) Charles X, but all of his virtues ac-
centuated his availability. He had a reputation for being
a hard bargainer, but the middle classes could respect his
business acumen. He knew how to spend wisely, as in the
reconstruction of the Palais Royal. His charities were well-
known. The Palais Royal, its gardens open to the public
and its salons hospitable to liberals and bourgeois, made
the Orleans family seem to belong to the people. The
Orleans sons attended a public secondary school—the first
time a princely family had made such a concession. Louis
Philippe must have been aware of the impression he was
making. A man with political ambitions would have behaved just as he was behaving, but in part his efforts may

have been motivated by the need to refurbish the Orleans name. The failure of the elder Bourbon line to reconcile the two Frances under the Charter made the Orleans family conspicuous as an alternative. There were "Orleanists"—a potential party—even though Louis Philippe would not admit that he was one of them.

— 3 —

THE JULY REVOLUTION

Background. France under the Restoration was in many respects well-governed. The finances were orderly. An indemnity to Napoleon's conquerors was paid and the foreign occupation ended in 1818. France served as agent of European order in suppressing a revolution in Spain in 1823. Mediterranean interests embroiled the French in the Greek cause where they helped bring about Greek independence from the Turks. Disputes with the dey of Algiers over piracy and commercial credits led in June, 1830, to the landing which was to end, after many trials, in the conquest of Algeria. At home the population passed 30 million in 1821. Still more than three-quarters rural, the country had not yet made up its foreign trade losses of the Napoleonic era, but was convalescing slowly behind protective tariff barriers. There was a fair degree of prosperity until the late 1820's.

The Restoration also had its dangerous side. Reconciliation of the nobles and middle classes was hampered by their competition for government jobs and places in the professions now that the more open society encouraged expectations in the educated middle class; the slow growth of the economy was not providing enough new opportunities. Birth and death rates were high, and the generations passed from the scene more rapidly than today. Only about 11 percent of the French of 1827 had been adults in 1789. Old wounds should have healed the more rapidly, one might suppose; but the new points of view clashed with those of the elders still in power, Charles X and his circle.

After 1826 there were hard times, as a commercial slump of that year was aggravated in 1827 and 1828 by agricultural depression. By 1830 the worst was over, but the economy was still unhealthy at the time of the July Revolution, and did not recover until 1832. The years from 1827 to 1832 were economically gloomy and socially uneasy.

Paris at this time was unusually prone to poverty, violence, fear, and class antagonisms. From a population of about 548,000 in 1801 it advanced to over 785,000 in 1831. Housing, employment, charities, sanitation, and law enforcement failed to keep up with this population growth, which was in large proportion made up of young, active, unattached males and of workers whose position above the swarms of beggars and criminals was always precarious. What Louis Chevalier calls a pathological urban condition must certainly have contributed to the events of the July Revolution of 1830, as it did to many lesser disturbances through the years.

The conjuncture of these various economic and social conditions with a full-fledged political crisis made it easy for some unrealistic decisions on the part of Charles X and his ministers to provoke a revolution in July, 1830.

Charles X, when he became king in 1824, was 67 but was still a regal figure and a true aristocrat. He was loyal and generous to his friends, gracious as a monarch, and able to inspire devotion in those who knew him well. Although he had been profligate in youth, he was now a religious and conscientious ruler. He was not well-educated, or even very intelligent. He comprehended neither the need for representative political institutions nor the extent to which he and his close advisers were out of touch with the new generation. He felt no obligation to allow the legislative chambers to choose ministers and make policies. On the other hand, he did consider it his duty to consult the deputies before making up his mind. This was the manner in which he interpreted the regime of the Charter and intended to preserve it.

With the changing times, people outside of the king's circle came to defend a more liberal interpretation of the Charter. Legislation such as the indemnity to the *émigrés* for their losses during the revolution, and events such as the disbanding of the National Guard in 1827 for shouting in favor of the Charter, encouraged the growth of a parliamentary opposition and of the idea that the Charter required greater collaboration between the ministers and the parliament. In August, 1829, the king tried to counter this tendency by forming a new ministry led by his friend Jules de Polignac, an upright but old-fashioned and very unpopular Ultra.

Polignac's ministry, busy with Greek affairs and with the expedition which was to conquer Algiers, did not clash immediately with the legislature. At the opening of the parliamentary session in March, 1830, however, the king's message stressed his rights. The Chamber's response, voted by an opposition majority ("the 221"), was to praise representative government and to ask for a ministry more in tune with its own opinions. Charles X dissolved the Chamber in May, 1830, but in new elections in June and July the *pays légal*—the small number of citizens permitted to vote—decided against the king and gave 274 seats to the opposition.

Charles X could have avoided a crisis by modest concessions to the victorious legislature, but he feared that one concession would lead to another, as in the case of his unfortunate brother, Louis XVI, and that he would lose all of his authority to the legislature if he gave up any of it. In his view the legislature and the *pays légal* who had elected it were a minority misled by rich newspaper owners. He thought that the general public was with him, and he was probably encouraged in this view by the news on July 9 that Algiers had fallen to the French.

To cope with the political situation as they viewed it, Charles X and his ministers prepared a set of ordinances which they issued on July 26, under article 14 of the Charter, a clause which permitted emergency measures in time of crisis. (1) The press was placed under severe restrictions. (2) The new Chamber was dissolved before it met, on the ground that the elections had been improperly conducted. (3) The number of deputies was reduced and the number of electors further restricted in a manner prejudicial to the middle classes. (4) New elections were scheduled for September.

News of the king's counterstroke began to spread in the late morning of July 26, 1830, when the four ordinances were published in the government newspaper, *Le Moniteur*. Owners of the opposition newspapers, now forbidden to publish without special permission, decided to defy the law the following day. Journalists, inspired by Adolphe Thiers, published a manifesto recommending disobedience on the ground that the king's ordinances were illegal. Merchants and manufacturers decided to close their shops the following day, a measure which would enable their workers to participate in street manifestations. Some of the deputies of the dissolved Chamber decided to hold a meeting the following day. Charles X, in residence at Saint-Cloud, to the west of Paris, went hunting. He had been assured that police and military precautions in Paris were adequate.

The Three Glorious Days, July 27-29, 1830. On Tuesday, July 27, 1830, several newspapers appeared without authorization. The police began to seize their presses and search for their writers. In the streets republican students agitated among the many idle workers and there was some rioting. Charles X sent Marshal Marmont to take charge of Paris when it became evident that more than ordinary police action would be necessary. Marmont, who was unpopular for having turned against Napoleon in 1814, set up headquarters in the Tuileries palace and by evening had placed troops at the danger spots in the city. There was some fighting, and a few persons were killed. The deputies met, but they did not want revolution. They merely directed the historian Guizot to prepare a protest against the ordinances. Although by midnight the city seemed to have calmed down, left-wing groups were planning an insurrection for the next day.

On Wednesday, July 28, the situation in Paris worsened. Students and workers had built barricades during the night in the poorer districts of the center and east. In the morning gunshops and isolated military outposts were seized. The City Hall and cathedral of Notre Dame were taken and from their heights the tricolor flag of revolution flew, while the great bell of the cathedral tolled. Mingled with politically conscious groups shouting slogans were reinforcements from the populace of the great, overcrowded city: rioters turning the tables against established society. Toward noon Marshal Marmont, caught in a real crisis, sent columns of soldiers to knock down the barricades made of paving stones, felled trees, and vehicles, and to fight the rebels, who retaliated with shots and projectiles from windows and rooftops. The troops moved through the hot July day, but the barricades went up again behind them in the narrow streets. The action was indecisive, and toward evening Marmont recalled his columns to the refuge of the vast Louvre-Tuileries palaces with their fortress-like interior courtyards. The forces returned weaker, many having been killed or wounded and many more having defected to the popular cause.

During this day the opposition deputies met again and were joined by Lafayette and the banker Laffitte. There was some talk of a provisional government under Lafayette, to check further disintegration of the crumbling Restoration settlement. Some minds turned toward the Duke of Orleans, who had prudently disappeared from view.

On the third day, Thursday, July 29, Paris appeared unconquerable as multitudes joined the insurrection and barricades went up by thousands. Important positions such as the Palais Bourbon (home of the legislature) fell to the insurgents. In the Place Vendôme, near the Tuileries palace, royal troops defected, forcing Marmont to shift his remaining men. During this maneuver insurrectionists broke into the Louvre from the east end and fired on the royal troops in the courtyards, who panicked and departed from the west end of the complex of buildings and retreated up the Champs-Elysées and, eventually, out of Paris. With the city in the hands of the insurrection, the deputies in the early afternoon clung to their position of leadership by naming a municipal commission and reviving the National Guard with Lafayette at its head.

About this time Charles X, at Saint-Cloud, met with his ministers (refugees, like his army, from Paris) and reluctantly agreed that a new ministry was necessary and that the ordinances would have to be rescinded. He sent word of his concessions to Paris, but the municipal commission and the opposition deputies stalled for time, demanding written proof. The next day Charles X's newly appointed prime minister himself carried the king's signature to the city but was unable to make himself heard. By this time the tug of war was between republicans and the Orleanists.

The Crown Changes Hands. Paris was an enormous armed camp, victorious and disorderly. On the left bank (south) of the Seine the Palais Bourbon was the meeting place of the Chamber of Deputies, whose remaining members leaned toward an Orleans solution, a "French 1688" which would forestall a republic. The Chamber of Peers, whose seat was the Luxembourg palace, also on the left bank, was indecisive and ineffectual. On the right bank (north) of the river and somewhat to the east of the Tuileries palace stood the City Hall, where the municipal commission favored a republic. Louis Philippe's town residence was the Palais Royal, also on the right bank and close to the Tuileries. He returned to it just before midnight on July 30.

When the crisis began with the publication of the ordinances, Louis Philippe was with his family at their Neuilly estate, to the west of Paris. During the "three glorious days" (July 27-29) he went into hiding, first on his estate and later in a nearby village. He had reason to fear being taken into custody by either King Charles X or the revolutionaries, although in fact neither side made the attempt. It is possible that he was in touch with Orleanists like Thiers and Laffitte, who were trying to convince the public that he would be a citizen king and a safeguard against radicalism. Certainly the Orleanists were worried lest Lafayette and the municipal commission proclaim a republic. On the morning of July 30, when the king's defeat was an accomplished fact, Thiers' statement of the case for Louis Philippe was posted in Paris, and Thiers went to Neuilly, where he was unable to see Louis Philippe but left a note and secured the assurance of the duke's sister Adelaide that the Orleans family would support the revolution.

Louis Philippe's behavior testifies to a certain agitation. However ambitious he may have been, he had spent a quarter of a century restoring the family fortune and honor after his father's entanglements in the great revolution; he must have been concerned, if not actually horrified, at the danger of a repetition with himself in the role of Philippe Égalité. On the other hand, the crisis could not be wished away. Opportunity for personal advancement was not the only consideration; failure to act might be the equivalent of choosing a republic, which would perhaps mean exile for the Orleans family and collapse of the Restoration compromise, and possibly another round of wars with a revolutionary France pitted against Metternich's Europe. Reasons such as these were to be a large part of the Orleans "case" in future debates, but some of them must have disturbed Louis Philippe after July 26, 1830, alternating with visions of the throne and, no doubt, awareness of his own undeniable competence. In any case he seems to have hesitated about leaving his hideout but finally accepted an invitation from the deputies to join them in Paris. (*See Reading No. 1.*)

The night of July 30 and 31 seems to have been a sleepless one for him. After reaching the Palais Royal at about midnight, he had an early morning conference with Mortemart, Charles X's newly appointed prime minister, and apparently assured him that he, Louis Philippe, would never accept the crown, and even seems to have made this promise in writing, only to ask for it back a few hours later. No doubt some of the deputies put pressure on him. Talleyrand, who lived near the Palais Royal, seems to have advised him to accept the throne. In any case, the morning of July 31 saw him accept, from the deputies, appointment as Lieutenant General of the Kingdom, and announce this fact in a proclamation to the French people.

On this Saturday morning of July 31, Charles X and his family, feeling unsafe, moved from Saint-Cloud to Trianon and then went on to Rambouillet in the afternoon. In Paris, Lafayette was being urged to put himself at the head of a republic, but he refused to do so, fearing that a republic would become too radical, as in 1792. There was still some question, however, whether the municipal commission and the street crowds would accept anything short of a republic.

The Orleanists had to act if they wished to take command of the situation. At about two in the afternoon, therefore, a procession of deputies, led by Louis Philippe on horseback, wearing the tricolor on his hat, went from the Palais Royal eastward for about a mile to the City Hall through the armed, victorious Parisian crowds. It was a necessary risk which paid handsomely. One shot could have ended Louis Philippe's career and changed the character of the next 18 years. Outside of the City Hall the crowds were especially hostile and there were cries of "no more Bourbons," but the doorway was reached. Inside was Lafayette, who might still carry the day for the republicans, but the general led Louis Philippe (or was led by him) onto the balcony overlooking the square and there embraced him as the two stood wrapped in the tricolor. There was a thunderclap of applause—for the flag, perhaps—but in the release of tension the republic's chances evanesced. (*See Reading No. 2.*)

During the first three days of August the drama of the July Revolution played itself out. Lafayette and the republicans, who had failed to get concrete guarantees from Louis Philippe, consoled each other with the assumption that he would follow their "City Hall program" and submit a new constitution to the sovereign people. Louis Philippe was to deny having made such a commitment. On Sunday, August 1, Charles X named Louis Philippe Lieutenant General of the Kingdom, but the latter declined to receive this office from him. The next day, Monday, the old king abdicated in favor of his grandson, the nine-year-old Duke of Bordeaux, and directed Louis Philippe as a member of the family to see that this new sovereign, Henry V, enjoyed his rights. (*See Reading No. 3.*) On Tuesday, August 3, Louis Philippe at a joint meeting of the Peers and Deputies announced the abdication but not the accession. That same day a ragged Parisian force set out for Charles X's residence at Rambouillet, which it approached toward evening. Charles X still had troops and artillery of his own, but chose to avoid bloodshed. Accompanied by white-cockaded guards, his son Angoulême (who had also abdicated), his grandson, the boy's mother (Duchess of Berry), and various retainers, he made a slow, dignified retreat to Cherbourg, where a rented American ship took the party aboard for transport to England.

Technically, Louis Philippe became king on August 9 in the presence of the two chambers, who two days earlier had voted for him and for a revised Charter. (*See Readings Nos. 4 and 5.*) The formalities were of some importance. Louis Philippe was called to the throne to fill a vacancy, instead of simply being proclaimed king. He was named King "of the French," not "of France." These niceties implied that he was something less than a king by inheritance; that he belonged to the nation instead of it to him. True, the nation was not consulted. A constitutional convention or even a referendum would have fanned the flames which the choice of Louis Philippe was meant to put out. The new king swore to uphold the Charter. For a while it had been supposed that he would be called Philippe VII, but in taking the name Louis Philippe I, he in effect acknowledged that he owed the throne to a revolution; his partisans adopted the illogical notion of "quasi-legitimacy," saying that the departure of the Bourbons created a vacancy which he filled in the public interest. For a time he tried to retain the *fleur de lis,* the arms of his family, even though it had been vilified during the revolution, but after further disorders he abandoned this link to the Bourbon past.

Louis Philippe wore the crown which belonged, said the Legitimists, to the boy whose rights he had failed to defend, the Duke of Bordeaux. Such a defense might have upset the delicate settlement by which the *pays légal,* with minor adjustments, preserved its preferred position for another 18 years. By being on hand, blameless for the original crisis, intelligent, and at the key moment energetic, Louis Philippe was able to serve his own interests and what his supporters thought was the public interest. These values he chose rather than the dynastic loyalty which would have involved him in a risky gamble for the preservation of the elder branch of the Bourbons.

The Charter Is Revised. The revised Charter published on August 14 no longer contained the preamble of 1814 in which Louis XVIII had claimed to be granting concessions of his own free will. By making this and other changes the deputies were in effect exercising the nation's constituent power. (*See Reading No. 6.*)

In the revised Charter, Catholicism was no longer called the state religion, but simply the religion of the majority of the French. This wording was a concession to the sensibilities of non-Catholics. There was also a guarantee never to reimpose censorship of the press. The king was no longer permitted to issue ordinances in emergencies, or to suspend the laws. Changes in the manner of choosing the peers and in the electoral law for deputies were promised.

The liability of the ministers to prosecution was no longer restricted to treason and peculation. The tricolor was made the French flag again, another link to the revolution.

The promised changes in the choice of peers and deputies came in 1831. On April 19 a new electoral law lowered the property qualification for voting from 300 francs to 200 francs of direct taxes (for a few persons of exceptional ability the requirement was lowered to 100 francs). The age for voters was lowered from 30 to 25 and for deputies from 40 to 30. The changes produced an electorate of 166,583 voters in 1831, which was to grow to 241,000 by 1847, owing to the increased prosperity of the country. The electorate of the Restoration had never reached 100,000. The *pays légal* of the July Monarchy was still clearly a plutocratic minority—less than 3 percent of the adult male population. To be eligible for office as a deputy, one had to pay direct taxes of 500 francs instead of the 1000 required under the Restoration. In the absence of an income tax, most voters and deputies under the July Monarchy qualified by paying taxes on real estate— still a favorite investment of merchants and manufacturers.

The upper house, the Chamber of Peers, was changed by a law of December 29, 1831, into a body whose members held office for life and were chosen by the king from certain categories of wealth and officialdom. The July Monarchy, despite the presence of an upper house, was less a compromise between aristocracies of birth and wealth than an opportunity for an aristocracy of wealth to try its hand at government.

The Public Acquiesces. Critics said that the Chamber had acted illegally because it had been elected as a legislature and not as a constituent assembly, but the French public cared little for such subtleties. Louis Philippe had imposed himself bravely by making the trip to the City Hall. Paris, and France, accepted this act. Without Lafayette as a rallying point the republicans were confused, and in any case they were largely middle-class intellectuals with scarcely any popular following. In 1830 there was no Bonapartist movement capable of competing with Louis Philippe. Napoleon I had died in 1821, and his son, the 19-year-old Duke of Reichstadt, was living at the palace of Schoenbrunn outside Vienna, under close watch of the

Habsburgs. His cousin Charles Louis Napoleon Bonaparte, the future Napoleon III, was now 22, but was yet to be heard from as a pretender. The last Bourbons of the elder line, Charles X and his family, aroused no great sorrow by their withdrawal. Their supporters, the Legitimists, many of them noble families who had been vacationing at their rural chateaux when the July Revolution took place, remained aloof from the new regime. They were a minority by whose alienation France was the poorer, but they represented no substantial threat to the July Monarchy.

Being a people's king meant receiving innumerable delegations, being summoned constantly to the windows, and having to sing the *Marseillaise* over and over. In the early days the Palais Royal was tramped through by thousands of visitors from all over France. This familiarity was unavoidable, for the Palais Royal was in the heart of victorious Paris, and months would pass, and even years, before the new regime could be called stable.*

* For the international repercussions of the July Revolution, see Chapter 8.

— 4 —

THE UNEASY YEARS

The economic dislocations lasted until mid-1832, aggravated by the violence of the Three Glorious Days and by the international crisis. Public disorders continued. (*See Reading No. 7.*) It was difficult to halt the revolution; the constitutional brake so swiftly applied had to be supplemented by the gradual tightening of police and military controls. Indeed, 1830 as an emotional and intellectual experience was indelible; the July Monarchy was never to erase the contradiction between its own limited assumptions and the popular and national inspiration which had been released. The new government did, however, demonstrate its will to rule by 1832, a year of unusual troubles, and then advanced toward firmer ground by 1836.

Palais Royal to Tuileries. Shortly after the July Revolution the Orleans family moved from the Palais Royal to the nearby and more sumptuous Tuileries. The Tuileries palace was to be burned during the fighting over the Paris Commune of 1871, but in Louis Philippe's time it stood across from the gardens which bear its name, joining the two arms of the Louvre which still point westward toward the Place de la Concorde. The new king and his family had a magnificent view up the Champs Elysées —toward the Arch of Triumph after it was completed in 1836. In that same year the Obelisk was placed in the Place de la Concorde, a gift of Mehemet Ali of Egypt.

The Orleans family in their new surroundings lived a relatively unpretentious existence suitable to a dynasty-by-consent. (*See Reading No. 9.*) Louis Philippe's personality lent itself to the role of people's king, although his intention was to direct the state's policies and to establish a solid hereditary dynasty. Before taking the oath as king he carefully transferred his great wealth to his children, reserving for himself only the income for his lifetime; he did not intend to have his property made into a crown domain. Later the Chamber confirmed this provision, but Louis Philippe was always criticized for it. The king had a quick temper, but it subsided quickly; usually cool and crafty in political maneuvers, most of the time he was friendly and talkative. He had an astonishing memory and was so well-informed that he was seldom boring even though he took a rather prosaic view of men and events. The *juste milieu* which he announced as his policy between the extremes of reaction and radicalism was entirely characteristic. By virtue of his judgment and experience he was certainly one of the ablest political leaders in France. He was self-confident and inclined to be impatient with his ministers. (*See Reading No. 10.*)

Because of public disorders and personal danger, Louis Philippe soon had to discontinue his walks in Paris and take his exercise where it was safer—inside the walls or at one of his country properties. His favorite recreation, architectural reconstruction, often took him to Versailles and Fontainebleau. This interest was intense, and it revealed his kingly ambition; he meant to be a monarch with the best in Europe, and spent great sums, including large amounts from his own fortune, on these projects. Although his taste has been the target of art historians, he made a lasting contribution to France's public monuments.

Assassination Attempts. The threats to Louis Philippe's life had little to do with majority opinion. The king's popularity is difficult to assess, but it is probable that he was accepted by most people without inspiring devotion. He was recognizably a good and able man, but he never made himself symbolic of the nation's pride and self-respect. The frequency of physical attacks on the king resulted from a number of circumstances: the intoxicating ferment of ideas, the decline of respect for royalty, the multiplication of revolutionary sects, the unmanageable diversity of the Parisian metropolis, the increasing importance of the press. In the arena of mass opinion, Louis Philippe's wealth, supposed avarice, and bourgeois appearance lent themselves to disrespectful jokes, cartoons, pamphlets, and scribblings on walls. Besides his portly appearance and umbrella, the pear (*la* *poire,* his heavy-jowled head) became famous. In those times of discontent and political inexperience such insults were dangerously provocative.

In November, 1832, Louis Philippe was fired upon while crossing one of the Paris bridges on horseback. The smoking pistol was recovered, but the young man who had probably fired it was acquitted for lack of evidence. The worst attempt on the king's life occurred on July 28, 1835, anniversary of the July Revolution, during a parade. A weapon consisting of some two dozen gun barrels bound together had been fired by a Corsican named Fieschi, who was put up to it by two minor Parisian revolutionaries. (*See Reading No. 16.*) All three were tried and executed. The episode shocked public opinion and facilitated the passage of the repressive "September Laws" (1835). (*See Reading No. 18.*) But Louis Philippe was scarcely any safer; reluctantly, he began to use an armored coach late in 1835.

The following June, as the king, the queen, and the king's sister were leaving the Louvre in the armored coach, a young man named Alibaud stepped up to it and fired from a gun disguised as a cane, barely missing his target. In December, 1836, Louis Philippe was shot at again, this time while on his way from the Tuileries to the Palais Bourbon. The young revolutionist missed, as his fellows continued to do all through the reign. But apart from the danger, which Louis Philippe faced with courage, these events hurt the July Monarchy by recalling its revolutionary origins and by making the regime appear more unstable than it really was. There were many false alarms, and it was impossible to know what to expect next. On one occasion a box mailed to the king from South America was opened by the police. It contained rattlesnakes, fortunately paralyzed by the cold.

Royal Pretenders. The Legitimist opposition was not extinct; many Legitimist papers were read in country chateaux whose owners, in some regions, were still influential. In the Chamber the orator Pierre Antoine Berryer and a few followers had taken the required oath of loyalty to Louis Philippe and were permitted to be a vocal opposition. Chateaubriand, technically a member of the Peers, was loyal to the elder branch mainly out of a sense of etiquette. The Legitimists were weakened by the desire of Catholics to separate their cause from that of the defeated monarchy of Charles X.

The most enterprising Legitimist was Marie Caroline, Duchess of Berry, who had left France in 1830 with her father-in-law, Charles X, and her 10-year-old son, the Legitimist pretender Henry V, in whose favor Charles X had abdicated. The duchess was still relatively young—32 at the time of her exile—and was as fearless as she was misinformed about the strength of her son's partisans in France. Expecting popular support, which never came, she landed with a few friends near Marseille in May, 1832, and then, rather than admit her failure to inspire a revolt, went in disguise to the Vendée, the old royalist stronghold in the west of France. Here an insurrection of some hundreds of peasants was defeated by government troops. Marie Caroline went into hiding in the city of Nantes.

The "affair of the Duchess of Berry" was extremely awkward for her "uncle Philippe," who was ridiculed for not catching her. He was reluctant to do so lest severe punishment make him look like a brute, or leniency seem a betrayal of the 1830 revolution. The duchess was finally arrested when someone lighted a fire in a fireplace behind which she was hiding. She was imprisoned in a chateau. Louis Philippe was faced with the distasteful prospect of a much publicized trial when he was saved by a miracle not unlike that of 1820. Pregnancy forced the intrepid young woman to announce a marriage which removed her from the political scene.

On July 22, 1832, the Duke of Reichstadt, son of Napoleon I, died at the age of 21. His passing seemed to end the Bonapartist threat. Napoleon's brothers were still living, but were inactive. A nephew, Charles Louis Napoleon, who in 1832 was 24 years old, inherited the role of pretender. His older brother had died in 1831, after the two boys had participated in a nationalist and liberal uprising against the Papal State. This episode, with its subversive *Carbonari* associations, gave Louis Napoleon the appearance of a romantic young radical. He and his mother tried to settle in France later in 1831, but Louis Philippe would not rescind the law exiling Bonapartes.

The Napoleonic legend was to grow stronger in the 1830's as a new generation discovered its charm and infused it with romantic enthusiasm. Gifted writers—Thiers, Balzac, Hugo, Béranger—gave Napoleon's figure a promethean grandeur. For a time after Napoleon's downfall romantic enthusiasm had turned toward the traditional, the Catholic, and the aristocratic, but by the 1830's a broader current was exalting more liberal and democratic versions of national self-esteem. The name "Napoleon" took on liberal and democratic connotations to match its nationalistic magic.

At the frontier city of Strasbourg in the early morning hours of October 30, 1836, Louis Napoleon tried to win over the garrison and march on Paris, but instead was arrested. In Paris Louis Philippe spent a nervous evening when the semaphor signals were interrupted by fog before the outcome of the coup was known. He then shipped his young rival off to the United States, leniently foregoing punishment which would have necessitated a trial with attendant publicity. The accomplices at Strasbourg were tried, but were acquitted by a jury: a rebuke to the July Monarchy, and publicity for Louis Napoleon.

Radical Reformers. The July Revolution revitalized ideas that had been successfully minimized since Thermidor, Brumaire, or Waterloo: the people's physical power and political potential; the nation as a supreme value; the French as liberators of other peoples; questions of social justice.

In the 1830's the republicans were reinforced by men disillusioned by Louis Philippe's dubious political claims or by the wholesale purging of officeholders which followed the change of regimes, or desirous of a more democratic suffrage, or a more spirited foreign policy. Republicans began to have better leaders: politicians such as G. Cavaignac and Etienne Garnier-Pagès, and journalists such as Armand Marrast and Armand Carrel. (*See Readings Nos. 11 and 15.*) The society *Amis du Peuple* had a mixture of democratic monarchists and republicans; its successor the *Droits de l'Homme* had subdivisions named after Robespierre, Marat, Babeuf, and other revolutionary forefathers. The republicans were learning about social problems, but socialism, the labor movement, and republicanism remained distinct from each other.

In the early 1830's socialist ideas seemed to be spreading, along with republicanism, but as the July Monarchy found its footing, these movements suffered setbacks and seemed about to disappear. They were to flourish again in the 1840's.

The first well-known socialist appeal was made by the Saint-Simonians. The master himself, Claude Henri de Saint-Simon, had died in 1825, but his disciples Armand Bazard and Prosper Enfantin attracted much attention in Paris with their public lectures and newspaper, *Le Globe,* and by living in a highly organized "family" with a few followers. They were not, however, a movement with mass support. Quarrels about rituals and whether free love was the best way to emancipate women discredited the Saint-Simonians, and when the government prosecuted them in 1832 as an illegal organization, and jailed some of them, they suffered an eclipse. But the Saint-Simonians left strong intellectual influences. Saint-Simon himself had seen the vision of industrial production alleviating the lot of mankind, and with his sense of history had appreciated scientific knowledge as evolved beyond earlier theological and metaphysical ways of thinking. His followers tried to work out in detail his idea that social arrangements and material rewards should be proportioned to service—to combine humanitarianism with economic development. Grasping at a science of society, they were more paternalistic than liberal and egalitarian. Some of them turned up later in the century as engineers and industrial promoters.

Charles Fourier (d. 1837) had a small and international following, most of them isolated individuals. In the early thirties a few colonies of Fourierists were attempted, and failed, but the basic criticism of savage economic competition, poverty, and war was not forgotten. Fourier wanted "association" in planned communities which would teach by example and spread through the world. The heart of his system was respect for the individual. Not just material welfare but psychological adjustment should be the basis for social organization; like Rousseau, he wanted civilization corrected so that individuals could be free and still cooperate with each other. This libertarian conception of social justice exerted a lasting charm.

Abbé Félicité de Lamennais was also rebuffed in the 1830's after a campaign to ally Catholicism with the new liberal tendencies. Under the Restoration, Lamennais had been an ultramontane who looked to Rome and deplored the privilegd, state-regulated position of the French Church under the Concordat of 1801. He developed the view that the Church, to maintain its proper moral influence, needed to be free of the state. He and his friends Jean Baptiste Henri Lacordaire and Charles de Montalembert founded the newspaper *L'Avenir* with the motto "God and Liberty," and tried to convince liberals and Catholics that they needed each other. Lamennais was applauded, but never had a large following. The French bishops opposed him, and Pope Gregory XVI failed to respond to his appeal in 1831 and 1832 and eventually condemned the liberal doctrines. Lamennais in 1834 published *Paroles d'un croyant* in which he insisted upon his democratic and republican views. He was excommunicated and became increasingly radical. (*See Reading No. 14.*) His Catholic friends did not follow him out of the Church, however, and a liberal Catholic movement persisted.

Public Disorders and Misfortunes. The July Revolution was followed by a brief period of great expectations, as had happened in 1789 and would again in 1848. This euphoria passed, by October or November, 1830, as everyday life and hard times resumed. Riotous Parisian crowds directed their hostility toward churches and priests, toward Charles X's captured ministers, and toward the representatives of foreign governments. Louis Philippe's new regime avoided an atrocity by spiriting Charles X's ministers out of Paris, but did not halt an outburst of church-wrecking which lasted for two days in February, 1831. As the months and years passed, labor troubles were mingled with the agitations of republicans and socialists.

Louis Philippe's government was not helpless, for the National Guard stood by it, but the early ministries, such as that of the banker Laffitte, were unable or reluctant to oppose the recently victorious Parisian populace. As soon as he dared, Louis Philippe got rid of Laffitte (and of

Lafayette as commander of the National Guard) and appointed a strong man, the banker Casimir Perier, to head the government.

Perier's ministry, from March 13, 1831, to his death on May 16, 1832, was of vital importance to the July Monarchy. He was the man who made it plain that the revolution was over. In Charles X's time Perier had been a member of the liberal opposition. Now he became the inspirer of the "resistance" to further change. Perier was a severe, irritable, willful semi-invalid with the gift of leadership. He said "no" to disorder at home and to the foreign crusading which the radicals advocated, and he also dominated the Chamber while making Louis Philippe stay in the background and reign rather than rule. The king resented him and privately referred to him as Casimir "Premier" but appreciated his value.

Perier's defense of order restored the confidence of bankers and foreign powers in the stability and peaceful intent of the regime. His policies (*See Reading No. 10*) are best illustrated by two serious crises. In September, 1831, news of the liquidation of a Polish uprising by the Russians led to riots in Paris, for French radicals wanted their country to defend freedom for other peoples. Perier suppressed the demonstrations. A second crisis concerned one of the classic cases of labor unrest in the 19th century, the uprising of the Lyon silk workers in November, 1831. The situation involved workers' efforts to check falling wages in depressed times. The government opposed wage fixing. The Lyon workers, with the help of local National Guard units, took over the city and launched the slogan "to live as free men, working, or die fighting." Perier in early December sent an army and recaptured the city.

Perier died in a cholera epidemic which ravaged France from March to July, 1832. Unsanitary, overcrowded Paris had about 21,000 victims. Among the ignorant there was a rumor that government agents were poisoning the wine in the poor quarters. There was also an insurrection of ragpickers against the government's efforts to improve sanitation. Following Perier's death in May, Louis Philippe took over direction of the government, but in June

ran into a violent insurrection typical of that era. Two
days of rioting resulted when the funeral of General
Lamarque, made into a political manifestation by Lafayette
and the moderate opposition, got out of hand. Louis
Philippe rose to the occasion and proved that he and the
National Guard could restore order.

With this victory and the almost simultaneous failure
of the Duchess of Berry's royalist insurrection, the waning
of the cholera epidemic, and the gradual lifting of the
depression, Louis Philippe's position was improved. Although 1832 was a significant turning point, it was not the
end of violence. In April, 1834, the republican *Droits de
l'Homme* society, which had avoided the law against unauthorized organizations by dividing into small cells, was
hit by a law against such subdivisions. (*See Reading No.
12.*) This legislation, which also hurt the rudimentary
labor organizations of those times, contributed to another
tragic uprising at Lyon, involving several days of fighting
and the use of royal troops and artillery. The republicans
of the *Droits de l'Homme* were only a small part of the
Lyon uprising, but they had cells in other cities, and
they attempted an insurrection in Paris, where a hope-
less struggle was engaged against regular troops and the
National Guard. In a cumbersome trial which began
a year later (April, 1835) sympathizers of the captured
republicans made use of the occasion to criticize the
regime, but neither side won the propaganda battle. Radicalism was discredited by the horrible spray of assassin's
bullets let loose by Fieschi in July, 1835 (see p. 35). The
repressive "September Laws" of 1835 outlawed provocative insults to the king or demands for a republic. (*See
Reading No. 18.*)

Apparently nothing could stop the ferment, for in
March, 1836, police uncovered a secret society called
"Families" based on groups of five people with false names
—in part remnants of the *Droits de l'Homme*. But by 1836
the regime was stronger than ever, and its opponents
weaker. The great majority of the population, peasants
and businessmen, were not revolutionary—1789 and the
Napoleonic Code had seen to that. In spite of the erosion
of Louis Philippe's never very deep-seated popularity, most

well-to-do and influential people were for him, the National Guard backed him, and the state's military and administrative personnel were loyal. Louis Philippe was winning the day-to-day contest and if he escaped assassination would have his chance to apply his conception of kingship to larger problems.

MEN AND POLITICS

In France's parliamentary development the years between 1830 and 1840 saw Louis Philippe navigating carefully toward a relationship of crown, ministers, and legislature which was to be the pattern of the 1840's and the final form of the July Monarchy.

Parliametary Life. Louis Philippe had to get along with the *pays légal,* the minority privileged to vote, and with their delegates in the Chamber of Deputies, whose assent to legislation was necessary, and who could propose laws. He also had to secure the agreement of the Peers, but under the July Monarchy the Peers were of little consequence. Appointed by the king for life, they lacked the prestige of an aristocracy and the authority of an elected body.

In the July Monarchy voting was considered a public function performed by a certain kind of person—one with the capacity to choose deputies to represent the national interest. In theory it was not the private interests of the voters that were being represented. The small electorate and smaller number of eligibles for office made for homogeneity and a high level of competence in the Chamber. On the other hand, the small electorate was vulnerable to pressure from the administration and was narrow in its outlook—about as good an example of class prejudices in politics as history provides. Most electoral districts had between 300 and 800 voters. The ballot was supposed to be secret but in practice was not. Deputies received no salaries; they had to be independently wealthy to be eligible. Civil servants could become deputies, and deputies could become civil servants without giving up their seats in the legislature.

In the restricted electorate and clublike Chamber per-

sonal influence counted heavily. Groupings were informal
and frequently changed membership when different issues
arose. Leaders fell into certain classifications, but their
personal ambitions and friendships seemed to count more
than doctrines, as was natural in a setting where almost
everyone agreed on fundamentals.

There were a few deputies known as *anti-dynastiques*—
that is, against the dynasty—against the whole regime of
the July Monarchy. Among them were a few Legitimists
and a handful of respectable and well-bred republicans.
The parties called *dynastiques* or "constitutional," who
were loyal to the Orleanists regime, are usually described
by historians as those of "resistance" and those of "movement." The "resistance" was against further constitutional
change. A Right Center led by the banker Casimir Perier
and a group of so-called Doctrinaires led by the historian
Guizot took the view that the revised Charter represented a
more or less permanent political settlement rather like
England's 1688. The parties of "movement" did not want
drastic changes but only a slightly broader suffrage and
somewhat more definite control of policy by the Chamber,
with less leadership on the part of the king and his spokes-
men. The "movement" is usually described as consisting of
two principal parties, the Left Center whose most famous
member was to be Adolphe Thiers, a journalist and historian, and the Dynastic Left led by Odilon Barrot, who
was to be the promoter of the banquet campaigns of 1848.

This conventional classification using the terms "resistance" and "movement" is not very useful, for the only
ministries of "movement" to hold office were those in
1830 and 1831; judged by their behavior, all of the remaining ministries may be labeled "resistance," including
two headed by Thiers. Judged by principles, the Dynastic
Left led by Odilon Barrot remained faithful to "movement," but in critical moments Thiers, of the Left Center,
spoke the language of "resistance." The fact is that none
of the "dynastic" or "Orleanist" political leaders ever produced a program of "movement" sufficiently inspiring to
establish relations of loyalty and mutual respect between
the parliament and the general public.

The usual means by which ministers and, less frequently, ministries were overthrown during the July Mon-

archy was defeat of the government during the discussion of the *adresse*. The *adresse* was parliament's response to the king's annual message, or *discours du trône,* and was debated clause by clause as if it were a law.

Legislation was sparse, but a few measures of lasting importance were passed during the early years. Elective councils were organized in local governments and planned for the colonies. A law sponsored by Thiers permitted property to be taken by eminent domain for public works, thus clearing the way for improvements in transportation. Guizot's education law of 1833 required local governments to provide primary schools and teacher training institutions.

Louis Philippe's Political Style. Under the Charter the king was commander of the military forces and could declare war and make treaties. Louis Philippe set great store by these powers, feeling himself well qualified by virtue of his command of languages and his unusual experiences in many lands. The king also shared the legislative initiative and could (but never did) refuse to sanction laws.

Louis Philippe had the right to appoint or dismiss ministers, and could choose them from within the Peers or Deputies. Ministers were subject to criminal prosecution if they broke the law. Otherwise they were the king's appointments, and not the legislature's. But after Charles X's disastrous experience it was agreed that ministers and their policies had to be acceptable to the Chamber as well as to the king.

In French political history the era from 1814 to 1848 witnessed several major tendencies. (1) Individual ministers with uncoordinated policies tended to give way to teams of ministers, i.e., ministries with unified sets of policies. (2) Responsibility of ministers to the king alone tended to give way to their responsibility to the parliament, as individuals and even to some extent as ministries. (3) The nature of responsibility came to be more clearly understood.

At first only *criminal* responsibility—liability to prosecution for breaking the law—was widely understood, and this was the sense in which the Charter of 1814 called ministers responsible. *Political* responsibility—the obligation of a minister or ministry to have policies acceptable to the parliamentary majority—was early recommended by a few theorists and under the Restoration came to be an article of faith of most liberals; it was contested by Charles X with fatal results in 1830, and afterward generally accepted without being clearly defined. The July Monarchy had an opportunity to root parliamentary practices in French political soil.

The revised charter of 1830 did not contain the idea of a homogeneous ministry, nor did it contain any clear-cut reference to the political responsibility of a minister or ministry. Louis Philippe was not obliged to appoint ministers *indicated by* the majority in parliament, but was expected to keep in office ministers *acceptable to* the parliament. Although either house could overthrow a minister or ministry, Louis Philippe enjoyed much freedom to exercise his political talents. The Peers never troubled him, and most of the time the Deputies lacked the organization, discipline, and solidarity to force their will upon him. In time, his freedom of action was increased by the building of a "palace party" of obedient deputy functionaries— deputies with other government jobs—and "individual conquests" who had been won over by government favors.

Louis Philippe wanted to do more than merely reign, if reigning meant appointing ministers capable of doing good work and getting along with the legislature. He did not mean to dictate to the ministers or defy the legislature, but he was determined to have a part in inspiring the ministry which led the Chamber and retained its confidence.

In the first months of his reign, as noted, Louis Philippe let the relatively popular men of "movement," Dupont de l'Eure and Laffitte, who had the valuable support of Lafayette, act as a buffer between the new government and the revolutionary crowds. These men failed to produce a coherent program or dominate the situation, and Louis Philippe was able to get rid of them. Lafayette died in 1834. The memorable ministry of Casimir Perier, from March, 1831, to May, 1832, did much to establish the practice of having a real prime minister and a cabinet identified with definite policies. Louis Philippe liked Perier's "resistance" policies, but resented being forced into the background to reign but not rule. After Perier's death he tried to preside over the ministers himself, but this practice tended to embarrass them and lose them the support of the Chamber.

Between 1832 and 1836 Louis Philippe was forced to rely, most of the time, on able prime ministers of some prestige and independence such as the aristocratic Duke of Broglie. From April, 1834, to March, 1835, he tried to replace Broglie with various "illustrious swords," military dignitaries without political preferences, but these men were unable to retain majorities in the Chamber. By 1836 Louis Philippe had reluctantly accepted the necessity of having a "president of the council," or prime minister, rather than fill that capacity himself. He was still determined to have a prime minister who would agree with his own policies.

Thiers. The first Thiers ministry, from February 22 to September 6, 1836, marked the end of a period when the king had been obliged to put up with the so-called "triumvirate" of Broglie and two able young historian-politicians, Guizot and Thiers. By appointing the ambitious Thiers, Louis Philippe separated him from his colleagues and inaugurated the famous Thiers-Guizot rivalry.

Adolphe Thiers (1797-1877), then nearing 40, was a small, aggressive, self-made man of near-genius, full of energy and ambition. He had appeared in Paris in the 1820's with a law degree from Aix-en-Provence and begun to make his way as a journalist and historian of the great revolution. With this start he attracted attention, moved in fashionable circles, and was one of the most influential backers of Louis Philippe in the 1830 revolution. He was a brilliant parliamentary debater with great clarity of mind, who was recognized to have unusual abilities but generally regarded as opportunistic. Never idle, he was to continue publishing his *History of the Consulate and Empire* from the 1840's to the 1860's in the intervals between political activities. He was an admirer of Napoleon, and people were amused by what they felt was his imitation of that other small-statured careerist.

Thiers' first ministry, the six months in 1836, constituted a brilliant, characteristic performance of balancing, for he had no real majority and no clear policy. He was finally trapped by a curiously combined foreign and domestic situation. When Louis Philippe felt able to seek friendlier relations with the eastern monarchs whose attitude was so important to his dynastic ambitions, a marriage alliance with the Habsburgs was sought. In the spring of 1836 Louis Philippe's oldest son, the Duke of Orleans, was on the verge of winning the hand of Archduke Charles' daughter Theresa, but Alibaud's attempt on Louis Philippe's life (June 25, 1836) made the Orleans throne seem insecure. Whether this was a pretext or not, the marriage plans fell through.

Thiers responded to this setback by becoming belligerently anti-Habsburg and urging military intervention on the liberal side in Spain, to oppose Metternich's policy there. At this juncture Louis Philippe canceled the intervention, kept his reputation as a champion of peace, and forced Thiers' resignation.

Parliamentary Maneuvers. Between 1836 and 1839 the prime minister was Count Louis Mathieu Molé, a peer who was committed to no party and was willing to serve the king's policies. It was a period of relative calm and prosperity. The marriage of the king's oldest son in the spring of 1837 to Helen of Mecklenburg-Schwerin, a Protestant from a respectable lesser German dynasty, took place in an aura of national good humor and was the occasion for the opening of the palace at Versailles, which the king had restored.

Molé could not have lasted so long if Louis Philippe had not at one point allowed him to reshuffle his cabinet and continue in office after a defeat in the Chamber. In 1838, despite the general prosperity of the country and the political somnolence of the public, there arose objections to the king's "personal government." Guizot, Thiers, and Barrot, leaders of the Right Center, Left Center, and Left of the Chamber, formed a coalition against Molé's fragile majority.

Early in 1839, the "coalition" made a supreme effort to overthrow Molé, who was accused of serving as an instrument for the king's personal rule. Throughout a bitter 12-day debate Molé retained his majority by a narrow margin, but at its close he felt obliged to offer the king his resignation. Louis Philippe dissolved the Chamber and took the fight to the country, but in spite of his and Molé's efforts the coalition won a majority; now Molé was definitely out of office (March, 1839).

There followed, from March 8 to May 12, 1839, a long crisis in which no cabinet could be formed. The leaders of the victorious coalition could not agree on the division of the spoils, and finally Louis Philippe was able to have a man of his own choosing, Marshal Soult, an "illustrious sword." Guizot and Thiers got nothing, and went back to writing history.

Revolutionaries and Reformers. Determination to end the political crisis was strengthened by fear of disorders which increased with the economic slump of 1839, effects of which lasted into 1840. The worst threat came from a clandestine group of revolutionaries, the "Seasons," on May 12, 1839. The *Société des Saisons* was an offshoot of the *Droits de l'Homme* of 1834. It was organized by the revolutionaries Blanqui and Barbès with the help of a printer, Martin Bernard, and aimed primarily at recruitment of laborers rather than students or soldiers. During the insurrection of May 12 about 600 men seized the law courts in the center of Paris, but were thrown back from the police headquarters nearby. Lacking mass support, they were then defeated by the National Guard. The leaders were eventually caught and jailed. Blanqui and Barbès were condemned to death, but the sentences were commuted to imprisonment. (For the various forms of radicalism, see Chapter 7.)

After the revolt of the "Seasons" Marshal Soult spent nine rather tranquil months in office but resigned in February, 1840, when the Chamber refused to provide a financial settlement for the Duke of Nemours, the king's second son, following his marriage. Thiers, with his capacity for surviving without a program or a solid majority, slipped into power again in what was to be a memorable ministry (March to October, 1840).

In 1840 the depression, strikes, and further street riots, which were severely repressed, helped stimulate a campaign for political reform. One target was the government's hold over deputies who were functionaries. This practice had been frowned upon during the revolution of 1789-1799, but had been used by Napoleon and permitted under the Restoration. The July Monarchy had a few inadequate precautions against deputy functionaries but the practice was common and was growing; there were 140 deputy functionaries in 1832, 150 in 1839, and 184 in 1846.

When the subject of deputy functionaries came up in the Spring of 1840, Thiers pulled from his hat a splendid diversion. It was time, he said, for Napoleon's remains to be returned to France. Joinville, Louis Philippe's naval officer son, should be sent with a squadron to fetch the coffin from the distant island of St. Helena. This spectacular project was duly approved. England's consent was secured by Guizot, who was at the moment ambassador in London, and the prince set forth in July.

Meanwhile, since 1838 and parallel to the Chartist movement in Britain, pressure to extend the suffrage had taken the form of petitions and banquets. In the Chamber on May 16, 1840, François Arago linked political and social reform together and said that the people were sovereign. Thiers was stung into a frank defense of the July Monarchy and its social order. "In constitutional language, when you say national sovereignty you are saying the sovereignty of the king, of the two chambers. . . . I know of no other national sovereignty." And, with respect to the social question: "If you say to the people that they can have welfare by changing the political institutions, you will make them anarchists. . . ." The banquets and criticisms continued for a time, but Thiers repulsed the electoral reform projects in the Chamber.

The Eclipse of Thiers. Shortly after the legislature adjourned, Ambassador Guizot, in London, was told that on July 15, 1840, the other great powers, Britain, Austria, Prussia, and Russia, had agreed on an ultimatum to Mehemet Ali of Egypt. Mehemet Ali, rebellious vassal of the Sultan of Turkey, was something of a protégé of the French. (For details, see Chapter 8.) The great powers had isolated France as if it were the morning after Waterloo. Louis Philippe was indignant. The aggressive Thiers did nothing to caution the strident French newspapers. Tension mounted as Louis Philippe and Thiers, hoping that Mehemet Ali could produce a *fait accompli,* refused to back down.

History does not wait for one topic to be completed before introducing another. On August 6, 1840, Louis Napoleon Bonaparte, encouraged by the progress of his uncle's legend, tried to invade France near the channel port of Boulogne. He was arrested, tried, and sentenced to life imprisonment at the fortress of Ham, in Picardy.

Between Louis Napoleon's miniature invasion and his sentence on October 6, the crisis over Mehemet Ali had been reached. Thiers was for sending a fleet to the Mediterranean, but Louis Philippe wanted no reckless adventures. If the king needed public sympathy just then, it was provided by a sixth clumsy assassin, who shot at him from behind a lamp post on October 15, and missed. In any case the king held to his peaceful foreign policy, and accepted Thiers' resignation. The replacement as prime minister, on October 29, 1840, was the familiar "illustrious sword" Soult, but Guizot, back from London, was Minister of Foreign Affairs, and it was in reality to be Guizot's cabinet all the way to 1848.

On December 15, 1840, in unusual cold, enormous crowds watched Napoleon's second funeral procession pass by. Under the dome of the Invalides, Louis XIV's home for retired officers, Louis Philippe heard his son saying, "Sire, I present to you the body of the Emperor Napoleon" and replied: "I receive it in the name of France." (*See Reading No. 22.*)

Guizot. François Guizot, the new Minister of Foreign Affairs, was suitably cautious in foreign policy, and in the months that it took to liquidate the Egyptian affair the king and his minister began to see that their political conceptions were very similar.

Guizot was 53 in 1840. He was of Protestant, bourgeois upbringing and combined religious beliefs with personal uprightness and respect for hard work and business enterprise. Under the Restoration he had been a journalist, Sorbonne professor, civil servant, and historian of the English 17th-century revolutions and of modern European history. Guizot looked with approval upon the rise of the middle classes and their demands for political rights. He was a Doctrinaire to whom the Charter was a guarantee that persons of capacity would govern; sovereignty did not lie in the people but in Reason, and Reason was available only to those who had reached a certain level of training and responsibility. The charmed circle of "capacity" was open to all who could prove themselves by accumulating property.

Guizot's interpretation of recent history was a useful one, enriched by the historical awareness which the best men of his generation possessed. He was very secure in his knowledge, rigid, and disdainful of other possibilities. (*See Reading No. 17.*) Genuinely accomplished and well-intentioned, he seemed cold and intellectually arrogant to his contemporaries, while to historians he was to be a controversial figure, much criticized as an intellectual who failed to apply to the current scene the quality of analysis which he had used in writing history. He and Louis Philippe arrived by different roads at an alliance which they defended with satisfied immobility while the rest of the country was moving beyond them.

— 6 —

INDIVIDUAL AND SOCIETY

Parliamentary life was a small part of existence; for most citizens other activities—even of the state—seemed more important.

The Importance of Bureaucracy. Under the July Monarchy the salaries of Catholic, Protestant, and Jewish clergy were paid by state subsidy, although minor sects were denied this aid. Napoleon's centralized administration of departments, districts, and communes, each with appointed officials, remained; in the 1830's communal and departmental councils elected by substantial local taxpayers were added. During the 19th century the police, like other officials, became more numerous and files of information increased. A national army drafted annual contingents chosen by lot.

These developments ran counter to liberal theories, which held that the state should interfere as little as possible with society. Yet it was in the nature of things that the state should grow more powerful, if only to provide the rudiments of safety and sanitation for a bigger, more heterogeneous population. And there were projects which even liberals wanted: canals and railroads, for example, which entailed eminent domain and, as things worked out, government planning and support.

Liberty and Equality. The charters of 1814 and 1830 guaranteed personal liberty, equality before the law, religious liberty, freedom of opinion and of the press, and private property. There was still a widely accepted distinction between "political" and "public" rights. Political activities such as voting or holding office were not rights in our sense but were functions performed by persons with special aptitudes. The rights which we would call "civil" were then called "public": they were the rights which belonged to everyone.

The charters of 1814 and 1830 permitted the nobles, traditional and Napoleonic, to keep their titles, but specified that no legal privileges went with them. Entailed estates and primogeniture had been abolished by the great revolution as violations of the rights of heirs to inherit equally. Napoleon had brought them back for some of his nobles, but they were curtailed after 1835.

Under both charters the individual was supposed to be secure against arrest and imprisonment except as prescribed by law, and the privacy of the home and of the mails was supposed to be respected. In practice, however, these forms of liberty were still violated. In the French colonies slavery was not abolished until the revolution of 1848. Under the July Monarchy debtors could still be imprisoned up to ten years. Persons wishing to leave their local communities had to get passports from the local governments—in principle a formality, but in practice a nuisance.

Jews had enjoyed equality as citizens since the last restriction against them had lapsed in 1818, but there was a certain amount of antisemitism stirred up by their success in business. The liberty of lesser, nonrecognized religious cults was not as secure.

In principle the law was supposed to punish abuses of freedom of the press, such as incitement to riot, instead of censoring publications in advance. In fact the virulence of press attacks on the regime, coupled with the many cases of violence, led to severe measures, especially the "September Laws" of 1835. (*See Reading No. 18.*)

The famous Le Chapelier law of 1791 outlawing associations of workers or employers was still in effect. Napoleon's penal code in 1810 had forbidden associations of more than 20 persons without government permission; in 1834 a Law on Associations tightened the rules. (*See Reading No. 12.*)

One of the liberties about which there was controversy was the freedom to teach, which meant the right to open private schools or for parents to send their children to such schools. Guizot's education law of 1833 was very generous about permitting Catholics to open private elementary schools, but attempts to solve the problem on the secondary level led to great controversies. This issue was not solved during the July Monarchy.

The Population. The French population grew as follows:

27,000,000 inhabitants in 1801;
32,500,000 inhabitants in 1831;
35,400,000 inhabitants in 1846.

The French birth rate was declining after about 1820:

305 births for 10,000 inhabitants toward 1830;
281 births for 10,000 inhabitants toward 1846.

The death rate was declining also:

255 deaths in 10,000 inhabitants toward 1830;
227 deaths in 10,000 inhabitants toward 1846.

In the first half of the 19th century the French population was still increasing and even increasing a little more each year. In spite of the declining birth rate, which meant that average parents were not having as many children, there were more parents to have children; the declining death rate was bringing about this result. France's population, however, was already growing less rapidly than Europe's population as a whole. The poorest wage earners continued to procreate abundantly, while the middle classes and the moderately well-to-do artisans were beginning to practice birth control. The theories of Malthus appealed to many economic liberals. Catholics, together with some economists and some socialists, took the view that economic development could provide for large families.

France's population was still widely distributed; rural districts remained overcrowded. Movement to the towns accelerated in the hard times after 1846, but the greatest migrations were to come after the middle of the century. Paris grew from 774,000 in 1831 to over 1,000,000 in 1846, but three-fourths of the French population remained in rural villages or small towns.

The Peasants and Agriculture. The great revolution had removed seigneurial dues, leaving many small frams as private properties. The inheritance laws led to subdivisions as the population grew. No miracle had improved the

peasants' knowledge of agricultural techniques or provided
capital for improvements; even on the remaining large
estates capital was in short supply and the level of agricultural lore was low. Poor transportation prevented the
formation of uniform national prices. Agricultural products
were protected by high tariffs, as were industrial products,
but most farmers made meager livings.

To be sure, some of the Legitimists, retired to their
estates, took an interest in new crops, tools, and methods,
under the stimulus of improving roads and markets. The
government, through its prefects, tried to improve agricultural techniques, and Guizot's primary education law
had some effects. Population growth forced marginal lands
into use; fodder crops and vegetables cut into the ancient
practice of letting the land lie fallow; livestock feeding and
breeding improved.

In general, however, the peasants remained a world
apart, isolated, suspicious of townsmen, and hostile to
change. They had become a conservative political and
social force, even though nearly half of them were still
renters, sharecroppers, or day laborers.

Commerce, Industry, Investment. The French guilds
had gone with the old regime, but home industry survived
in force, along with numerous artisans and small busi-
nesses. High tariffs in the Restoration and July Monarchy
helped keep traditional methods alive. The road system,
until the 1840's, was a handicap. Mass transport was by
water, with steamboats on the rivers and nearby seas, but
with sails still dominating the oceans. The July Monarchy
continued a canal-digging program, at state expense. The
state also obtained the railway rights of way and built
the roadbeds, bridges, and tunnels, later leasing the lines
to private companies who furnished rails, trains, stations,
and working capital. This arrangement resulted from a law
of 1842, after earlier attempts of private concessionaires
had foundered. The first freight railway was in operation by
1833, and the first passenger line, from Paris to Saint-Germain, by 1837, but the big scramble for concessions, the
first major lines, and the public excitement over railway
shares came in the 1840's. Industry was largely family-
owned and self-financed from profits. Banking facilities
were not yet plentiful, although various thinkers including

the Saint-Simonians saw the need to link banking to industry. Loans to businessmen became more commonplace in the 1840's. So too did sales of stock, although limited liability required government permission unless the purchasers agreed to be inactive partners.

France's national monetary income increased significantly during the July Monarchy, and the supply of capital must also have grown—perhaps as much as 100 percent between 1820 and 1848. Perhaps 10 to 12 percent of the national income was the annual average rate of investment between 1820 and 1848. During the July Monarchy, France almost certainly achieved regular economic growth by making production outstrip population.

The most substantial changes in industry during the July Monarchy occurred in textiles, where machinery was changed from wood to iron. Despite the slow development of transportation and the distance of coal and iron deposits from each other, French production of coal increased sevenfold between 1815 and 1848. Production of pig and wrought iron was increased fivefold. France was able to make a large part of the rails and locomotives needed for the railroad building of the 1840's. Paris in 1848 was the world's greatest manufacturing city, with more than 400,000 industrial workers of all kinds.

Prices, Wages, and Labor. In the years from 1820 to 1848 France's national monetary income rose by perhaps 1.5 to 2 percent per year, while population was increasing by about .5 percent per year and prices were falling. Wages were falling too, but somewhat less rapidly than prices. At a glance, one would expect that real wages must have improved somewhat.

The focus needs to be sharpened, however, if the lot of particular groups is to be considered. The peasants were doing little more than hold their own against the population rise. Food prices tended to hold firm or rise slightly, and since wages, over-all, were declining, the economic condition of the wage earner tended to worsen, the more so because in those days he spent a large proportion of his income for food. Still greater precision would demonstrate that both wages and prices fluctuated and that periods of slump and prosperity affected employment. Some of the older, skilled trades held their own rather

well, but many workers in home industry were hard-pressed
by factory competition. Regional differences complicated
the picture. With all due caution, one may conclude that
under the July Monarchy wage laborers lived close to
subsistence and were under considerable tension owing to
wage, price, and employment fluctuations.

The economic fluctuations may be recorded in tabular
form if a detailed description is omitted.

1827-1830	Economic slump	Thus the years 1827-1832 make a rather long economic crisis, which should be remembered in connection with the political developments.
1830-1832	Recovery	
1833-1838	Relative prosperity, except for slump in textiles in 1836	
1839	Economic slump	
1840-1844	Recovery and relative prosperity	
1845-1847	Economic slump	Relevant to 1848 revolution, though indirectly

The principal labor crises as shown by clusters of strikes
in which the government took repressive action occurred
in 1831, 1833, 1840, and 1848. Employers lowered wages
in hard times, and workers sometimes struck in protest,
or waited until times were better and then tried to recover
what they had lost. In the July Monarchy there were some
attacks on machines in the manner of the English Lud-
dites, especially in 1830 and 1831. Violence, as at Lyon
in 1831 and 1834, was the exception; for the most part
workers who struck did not fight the authorities.

Nonagricultural manual laborers and their families
numbered about 4.3 million (13 percent of the total population) in 1826, and perhaps 6.3 million (18 percent of
the population) in 1848. The most numerous and generally the best-off were the old-fashioned skilled artisans
who were self-employed or worked in small shops and
lived in the older quarters of the towns and were neigh-
bors with several levels of bourgeois. These handicrafts-
men, reminiscent of the *sans culottes* of the great revolution, had their own traditions and values and were alert,

self-respecting people. Next in size after the artisans' shops were the many small factories in which groups of artisans or unskilled workers were employed, with few machines or none at all. And next came larger establishments using machines served by teams of workers, including women and children. Most factories were small, even those with machines. Many operations, particularly in textiles, were still done in home industry.

Despite the persistence of artisans, a new kind of working population was forming, chiefly from rural overflow and the high birth rate of urban wage-earning families. Certain streets were being invaded by wage earners who overcrowded the buildings and lowered the general level of neighborhood behavior, although landlords were profiting. Around the edges of Paris and other great cities, outlying villages were being turned into working-class suburbs. These people were generally poorer than skilled craftsmen, although better off than workers in home industry. Unlike the artisans, the factory workers were having to make a new culture in conditions of overcrowding at home and 14-hour days at the shop, with generally low wages and usually no reserve against sickness or unemployment. Until 1840 normal hiring was by the day, with the most favored being employed by the week. There was no social security. Periods of unemployment were frequent. Many working-class districts saw an upsurge in drunkenness, prostitution, and illegitimacy, and their mortality rates tended to rise. In large measure, the churches failed to hold these people in their new environments. Patterns of courtship, marriage, and child rearing changed; unions without marriage were frequent, with the woman less subservient and the children under less control than in bourgeois families—not surprising when women and children were wage earners. (*See Reading No. 27.*)

Under these conditions a class was forming, but it would be a mistake to overestimate its maturity during the July Monarchy. Wage workers were of many kinds and were little conscious of what they had in common. Consiousness and efforts at organization existed almost exclusively among the skilled craftsmen.

Compagnonnages of skilled artisans were illegal but were tolerated by the authorities. They had an old tradition. The young craftsman, taking to the road and working in town after town while gaining experience on his *tour de France* was looked after by the brotherhood. To some extent *compagnonnages* helped to maintain standards of employment and workmanship, but it is difficult to know whether they were inhibiting a modern labor movement or evolving into one. Another form of association was the society for mutual assistance, likewise tolerated by the authorities, but it reached only a minority of enlightened artisans. Mutual aid societies sometimes hid illegal "resistance societies" aiming at collective action through negotiation or strikes. Finally, there were a few efforts to form producers' cooperatives.

Napoleonic legislation had favored employers in cases of conflict over wages and had provided heavier penalties for labor leaders than for employers who broke the law against associations. The *livret,* dating from 1803, was a worker's paybook and passport and was supposed to be in good order before the worker was hired. The *livret* did not become obligatory in all trades, however. In theory the state's role in labor disputes was simply to keep order and enforce the laws. The courts were often mild toward labor in calm periods but in periods of labor unrest they were harsh toward labor leaders. The few employers' associations which existed were treated with leniency. There was virtually no labor legislation. A law of 1841 forbade employment of children under eight and restricted the workday of ages eight to twelve to eight daylight hours, and of children from twelve to sixteen to twelve hours, but it did not apply to small factories and had no adequate provisions for enforcement. Until the 1840's the Paris press treated strikes as news items without bothering to examine their economic and social backgrounds. The year 1840 saw the appearance of a labor paper, written by laborers, *l'Atelier,* which demanded radical changes in society. (*See Reading No. 21.*)

The Middle Classes. France of the July Monarchy was not ruled by a single middle class but by men the majority of whom came from a small top layer sometimes called *la grande bourgeoisie,* or upper-middle class. The upper-middle class is well illustrated by Casimir Perier, Louis Philippe's resolute prime minister of 1831-1832.

Perier's father and grandfather had been wealthy businessmen; the father had been a deputy under the Consulate
and a Regent of the Bank of France. Casimir Perier was
himself a banker and businessman; he succeeded his father
and an older brother as a regent of the Bank of France.
The Periers were one of the so-called "bourgeois dynasties," the families of greatest wealth and influence after
the great revolution. The top layer were financiers and
industrialists, with great merchants and lawyers following
close behind. There were also administrators at the higher
levels of government service, and some men of letters
such as Guizot and Thiers. All were wealthy, but not quite
all had inherited wealth or come from middle-class families. Thiers, for example, came from a very modest background. For persons of ability and connections it was
possible to join the upper-middle class, whose leaders
made use of a wide clientele. The ruling circles in the July
Monarchy were not identical with the 18th-century bourgeoisie; there had been many changes of fortune since
1789. But by the time of the July Monarchy the most
substantial families tended to intermarry and form profit-
able business and political associations and hold at arm's
length all but the most promising aspirants.

The July Monarchy with its restricted electorate was a
unique opportunity for this aristocracy of wealth, an opportunity which never returned. Under the Restoration
the older landed aristocracy had been predominant in the
government, the army, and the Church; the wealthy middle class had become electors almost by accident, because
payment of the *patente*, a business licensing tax, qualified
them to vote. The slightly broadened suffrage of the
July Monarchy assured the predominance of the upper-
middle class. The peasants and industrial laborers were
not politically conscious enough nor well enough led to
disturb the near monopoly of these leading families in
government, the administration, the Church, and the university.

Without the support or at least the toleration of "middle-
middle class" and lower-middle-class majorities in the
cities, Louis Philippe's regime could not have lasted. Large
numbers of small factory owners, merchants, professional
men, middle bureaucrats, small retail shopkeepers, and

commercial and government employees, shading off into the swarm of skilled self-employed artisans—all these generally approved of the Revolution of 1830 and disapproved of the disorders that followed. They were alert, active, hard-working, practical people, still primarily local and professional in their interests. It is impossible to say how much political consciousness they had. Although they did not get the vote in 1830, many of them hoped for further political changes. The National Guard gave them a sense of participation. Service in the National Guard was in theory obligatory to all taxpaying citizens, but those who could not afford uniforms and equipment were called "reserves" and not required to participate; the rest served willingly and with a sense of fraternity and patriotism, even though most them could not qualify as voters.

The mentality of the middle classes is suggested by the words orderliness, work, economy, and morality. The bourgeois family's property was passed from generation to generation, carefully divided according to the civil code; the children were guaranteed equal treatment; the wife and mother, legally incompetent, gave her chief attention to the household and children. There was confidence in material progress and in existing social institutions. It is difficult to assess the strength of religious faith, but Voltairean skepticism was less fashionable than it had been in the past.

— 7 —

VALUES AND ARTS

France, like Europe, was awakening from the spell of
the quarter century which had ended at Waterloo. The
great revolution and its aftermath had compelled a re-
assessment of the Enlightenment. For a time an international jury of kings and aristocrats had seemed to re-
enthrone tradition, but the attractions of secular progress
through science were irresistible. New evidence from the
industrial revolution was enriching the spectrum of ideologies.

Romanticism is the broadest term suggesting the style
and mood of the times, which honored energy, individu-
ality, and bold searching for new answers; there was also
a certain subjectivity, as men and women tried to be themselves and not copy previous generations. France had had
prophets to announce these values even before the revolution—Rousseau is an example. Paradoxically it was not
until after Waterloo that the French, whose exploits had
inspired Europe with wonder at the complexities of time
and change and with awe at man's capacity for good and
evil, themselves made a vogue of Romanticism. Returning
émigrés contributed to these influences. Romanticism was
full-blown in France by 1830 and declined in the late
1840's.

Literature. In literature the Romantic movement was
an emancipation from the rules of Classicism, within
which it was no longer possible for the new generation
to express itself. Greater liberties were taken with subjects,
vocabulary, and descriptions of inner experience.

Victor Hugo's play *Hernani,* which opened in Paris
on February 25, 1830, is often cited as a victory of the
Romanticists over the Classicists. His *Notre-Dame de
Paris* (1831), a novel about the city and the cathedral,

displayed the author's rhetorical contrasts and pictured swarming multitudes of people, as he was to do later in his lengthy series of novels, *Les Misérables,* published in the 1860's but in part written during the 1840's. Victor Hugo lived until 1885, moving, politically, from conservative royalism to republicanism and humanitarian concern for the lower classes. As an artist he was to be honored most for his poetry, which reached its full maturity in the 1830's.

Among outstanding literary events was another novel of the year 1831, *Le Rouge et le Noir* by Stendhal, a pen name of Henri Beyle—a pioneer in the description of psychological states but also a great story-teller, a Napoleonic veteran admirably fitted to describe the new 19th-century competitive society. Another series of literary events from the early 1830's to his death in 1850 was the publication of Honoré de Balzac's great sequence of novels, the *Comédie humaine,* exhibiting the social variety of France. Chateaubriand's *Mémoires d'outre tombe,* published after his death, from 1848 to 1850, were written between 1811 and the early 1840's. Chateaubriand was something of an historical relic, like Sieyès and Talleyrand, and indeed, Louis Philippe himself, but in literature he had set the new generation on its path. The great literary critic, Charles Augustin Sainte-Beuve, was already writing weekly articles during the July Monarchy.

Alphonse de Lamartine gained fame for his poetry in the 1820's and 1830's and then turned to politics and history. Théophile Gautier never abandoned poetry but also wrote exotic tales, and was a hard-working journalist. Alfred de Vigny, besides being a poet, was a pioneer of the historical novel. Alfred de Musset was a poet and dramatist who wrote *Confession d'un enfant du siècle* (1835) and other novels. The best-known composer of popular songs was Jean Pierre de Béranger; his topical political songs were highly critical of the regime and contributed to the Napoleonic legend.

Among popular novelists, Alexandre Dumas the elder turned out hundreds of works of fiction, including the *Trois mousquetaires* (1844). Like Eugène Sue, the widely read author of *Mystères de Paris,* Dumas wrote serials for the newspapers. George Sand, a woman whose real name was Aurore Dupin, was also a very prolific writer. In the 1830's her favorite theme was the misunderstood woman, but in the 1840's she turned to social problems. Prosper Merimée became noted for his *nouvelles,* or long short stories. Some of the best literature of the period was the work of historians and social critics.

The French Musical Scene. Paris was a great music capital, drawing to it Rossini, from Italy, and Meyerbeer, from Germany. Chopin, an international figure, who was brought up in Poland, although his father was French, was a pianist and composer who opened a whole new world for the piano. He was on the French scene much of the time, as was Liszt, the Hungarian virtuoso, one of the creators of the symphonic poem. The Frenchman Auber composed many operas. Scribe was a master of the libretto and contributed to many theatrical successes. The French composer Berlioz reached maturity in the July Monarchy with the performance, among other works, of his *Symphonie fantastique* (1830) and his *Damnation de Faust* (1846). Berlioz was one of the most original and profound of the romantics, whose genius at creating brilliant orchestral effects and whose influence on others— his use of the recurring theme, for example, which developed into Wagner's leitmotif—long obscured for some the substance and greatness of his work.

Fine Arts. In Louis Philippe's reign the Academy of Painting and Sculpture and its school, the Beaux Arts, were still devoted to the neoclassicism which Jacques Louis David had exemplified during the great revolution and the era of Napoleon. Neoclassicism, which deferred to the ancients concerning beauty and found in their literature the most edifying subjects, was represented after David's death by Jean Auguste Ingres, a fine draftsman and large canvas painter of historical subjects, as well as an excellent portraitist. The romantic revolt against neoclassicism was underway from the 1820's, however. After Géricault's death in 1824, its leadership was taken over by Eugène Délacroix, who painted both topical scenes and exotic faraway stories, and whose *The Barricades,* or *Freedom Leading the People* (1831) was about the July Revolution. The period of the July Monarchy was full of approved academic painters (many admired by Louis Philippe) who have since been forgotten. An outsider unable to get his canvases exhibited in the early 1840's was Gustave Courbet, a "realist" who claimed to reject both the abstractness of Classicism and the exoticism of Romanticism. The painter and sculptor Honoré Daumier left unforgettable political and social caricatures.

David d'Angers in 1833 finished the sculptured pediment on the front of the Pantheon, the *Patrie* distributing crowns to France's great men. When the Arch of Triumph, begun under Napoleon, was completed in 1836, one of its most striking sculptures was François Rude's "Le Départ" or "La Marseillaise," celebrating the defense of the nation at Valmy in 1792.

Romanticism produced no new architectural style, but there were many copies of Gothic churches. The architect Eugène Viollet-le-Duc, who was to be famous for many Gothic restorations, was still a young man when a law of 1841 ordered the restoration of Notre Dame de Paris, but it was Viollet-le-Duc and his team of artists and artisans who finished the project in 1864. The fashion for Gothic architecture influenced interior decoration. "Louis Philippe" furniture was, however, a comfortable modification of the Empire style.

Religious Values. In the broadest sense it was a current of religious feeling which swept along rebels like Lamennais (see Chapter 4); liberal Catholics like Lacordaire, whose sermons in the cathedral of Notre Dame in 1835 enchanted thousands; supporters of the Catholic missions were revived during the pontificate of Gregory XVI (1831-1846); ultramontane followers of Louis Veuillot, who became editor of *L'Univers Catholique* in 1842; the Protestant revival which was underway by the 1830's; socialists such as Pierre Leroux, Philippe Buchez, and the Saint-Simonians.

The Catholic Church, no longer discredited by association with the Restoration monarchy, was probably strengthened by Romanticism, the decline in fashion of Voltairean rationalism, and fear of radicalism. To be sure, conventional behavior was not proof of inner conviction; nor should one forget the loss to the Church of large numbers in the lower classes. There were bitter quarrels about Jesuits and whether Catholics should be allowed to set up their own secondary schools (see Chapter 9); back of these conflicts was genuine concern about the guidance of future generations. Religious concerns were especially manifest in the 1840's and contributed to the richness of that decade in searches for personal and social orientation.

The current of Catholic thought which is usually called traditionalism retained a certain influence. Its themes had been powerfully stated during the great revolution by Joseph de Maistre and Louis de Bonald, who brought history, science, and sociology together in support of the traditional European society and ultramontane Catholicism. Chateaubriand, the leading Legitimist man of letters, gave traditionalism and religion great aesthetic appeal. Some Catholic traditionalists proposed measures for the amelioration of working conditions and the avoidance of class struggle. An example is J. P. A. de Villeneuve-Bargemont's book *Economie politique Chrétienne* (1834), which anticipated what would in the 1890's be called "Social Catholicism." (*See Reading no. 13.*)

Philosophy and the Sciences. Academic philosophy in the July Monarchy was dominated by Victor Cousin, founder of the so-called eclectic school. Cousin and his followers tried to continue the Enlightenment's emphasis on reason as the criterion for truth, while at the same time taking account of all human possibilities—sensations, will, mystical experience. This was the analysis of the human condition to which Catholics objected when it permeated university and secondary teaching.

Catholic traditionalism and eclecticism both had their dissidents who cannot be recorded here. A third major current was positivism, represented by the publication between 1830 and 1842 of Auguste Comte's *Cours de philosophie positive* in six volumes. Posivitism was a set of conclusions about how to obtain reliable knowledge, interpret the past, and organize a morally acceptable society in the future. Like Saint-Simon, whom he served as secretary and disciple between 1818 and 1824, Comte placed the Enlightenment in perspective by explaining that many of its beliefs were based on principles which could not be tested. The task of the 19th century was to develop a final stage, the positive, or scientific, whose explanations would be in terms of testable conclusions. Comte thought that other sciences had reached the stage of positive knowledge and that the time had come to perfect the science of society, sociology.

Comte lived until 1857 and made detailed plans for the practical reorganization of society, capping his system with a religion of humanity. He was not by any means a radical or socialist in the usual sense. He was not egalitarian or democratic; the society which he envisaged was one in which do-nothings in high positions would be replaced by creative people, all for the good of humanity, to be sure, but Comte's social order had a medieval look which shocked John Stuart Mill and other former sympathizers.

Scientific education, valued as an agency of progress, was on the increase. Ideas of evolution of the universe and of living beings were becoming familiar to intellectuals. Ernest Renan, the rationalist historian of religions, grew up in the July Monarchy and in 1848 wrote an optimistic manuscript, *L'Avenir de la science,* which he was not to publish until 1890. Yet "scientism," the disposition to grant prestige to science, was not yet the mass phenomenon it was to become later in the century.

History. The passing of the old regime had stimulated historical curiosity and provided large canvases. Romanticism and its themes of time and evolution, its taste for particulars, its interest in the middle ages, and its revaluing of sentiment stimulated interest in history. Nationalism added incentives. Investigations of philology, folk tales, and legal systems made their contribution, as did the historical novels of Walter Scott and the plays of Shakespeare, at last triumphant in France. History and literature were still branches of the same art, but erudition was progressing.

François Mignet, who, like his friend Thiers, had already written about the French Revolution, went on to become a meticulous historian of the early modern centuries. Guizot's *Histoire de la Révolution d'Angleterre* (2 vols., 1826-1827) as well as his earlier *Essais sur l'histoire de France* (1823) and his published lectures on civilization, pointed the way to the critical study of documentary sources. Guizot wrote little between 1830 and 1848, but used his political influence to organize historical studies and publish documents at state expense. After 1848 he returned to historical writing. The medievalist Augustin Thierry pioneered in the use of original sources but remained a brilliant narrator. In style as in sympathy for the rise of the Third Estate he foreshadowed Michelet. The early volumes of Jules Michelet's *Histoire de France* were published between 1833 and 1844 and his seven-volume history of the French Revolution began to appear in 1847. Thiers' many-volumed history of the Consulate and Empire began to appear in 1845, and in 1847 came Lamartine's history of the Girondins, and Louis Blanc's long history of the French Revolution. These publications contributed to the "spirit of 1848," just as the historical studies of the 1820's had helped prepare the atmosphere for 1830. Michelet was a democrat and a nationalist with a mystical faith in the genius of the French people. Thiers was temperamentally suited to bring out the best side of Napoleon. Lamartine was captivated by the democratic aspirations of his subjects the Girondins. Louis Blanc as a social reformer had popularized the phrase "organization of labor."

Alexis de Tocqueville's *De la démocratie en Amérique* appeared in four volumes from 1835 to 1840. The author was aware that the interest in his subject stemmed from an inescapable trend toward democracy and social leveling in Europe as well as in America. He was to write about France in *L'Ancien Régime et la Révolution* (1856).

Conservative Ideologies. If an ideology is a collection of related ideas and attitudes propagated by believers, the royalist movement in Louis Philippe's time had several ideologies. Legitimism was a continuation of the ideology of the Ultras of the Restoration, and was related to the Catholic traditionalism already mentioned. To justify traditional institutions, it drew on science, positivism, and history, as well as on religious arguments. The historical process could be appealed to as a kind of reason, and social facts such as the family, the profession, and the geographical region could be used to counter rugged individualism and class warfare. Representative government could be hitched to established groups, and social distinctions could be defended as functional. Some of the Legitimists, including Chateaubriand and the orator Berryer, recommended extension of the suffrage in an effort to swing Legitimist royalism into the camp of progress, but the Legitimist movement was split by factions and failed to develop a popular program.

Liberal Ideologies. Until 1848 there was a certain vagueness about the liberal ideology. Partisans of political liberty for the middle classes rubbed elbows with partisans of the people, admirers of the revolution with admirers of the Empire, believers in *laissez-faire* with advocates of social reform.

The dominant form of liberal ideology in the July Monarchy may be called Orleanism, after the dynasty, even though it was not created by Louis Philippe and was to outlast him. The term covers fairly well the views of Perier, Guizot, Thiers, Broglie, and their colleagues in the ministries and chambers, in spite of their personal rivalries. These men accepted the political regime and social structure of the July Monarchy as a normal outcome of the revolution of 1789 and of all French history. They considered these arrangements to be a *juste milieu* or golden mean between reaction and revolution; they thought that a way had been found to have liberty and order, change without revolution. (*See Reading No. 30.*) Guizot is often scoffed at for thinking that history had ended with the July Revolution; he was not so blind as to suppose that there would be no further developments, but he thought that parliamentary government reflected interests, and that if economic change produced new interests they would be represented. This is the meaning of his much criticized *"Enrichissez-vous par le travail et l'épargne"*— "Enrich yourselves by work and by saving." If you want to share in political power, he was saying, you can prove your capacity by economic success.

The implication of this famous advice was that those who had ability and would work and save *could* rise in the world, while those who did not rise were lacking in some way. This social philosophy was criticized in its own time and has been criticized ever since for complacency about the fairness of the existing institutions. Orleanist liberalism was "conservative" in the sense that it defended the political and social order which had replaced the old regime. It was liberal in its rejection of the old regime, against which it had successfully defended certain liberties —for parliament, for the press and education, for the individual, for the economy. Yet the Orleanists interpreted political liberty narrowly and did not allow economic liberty to interfere with the high protective tariff. Freedom of thought and religion were protected, but the press was censored and public meetings and associations were restricted. The Orleanists believed in reason and education and were at times mildly anticlerical, but they did not wish to quarrel with the Church. In foreign policy there were differences of opinion—witness Louis Philippe and Thiers—but on the whole the Orleanists were nationalistic in their words and cautious in actual conduct.

A more democratic liberalism was that of Alexis de Tocqueville, who served as a deputy in the last years of the July Monarchy. Tocqueville was a noble and a landed aristocrat and a solitary, prophetic intellectual, not very effective as a politician but a profound analyst of the institutional changes taking place underneath appearances. His family background was Legitimist. He himself was to serve briefly as a minister under the Second Republic. Tocqueville has been claimed by both liberals and conservatives. Whatever one chooses to call him, he was a moralist who appreciated the effects of institutional changes on people, and he predicted and accepted the advent of democracy, fearing all the while its effects on liberty. If democracy was to be made compatible with individual rights, the people would have to learn responsibility and political judgment. Local training grounds would have to be provided through administrative decentralization and encouragement of group activities. These ideas were not fully formulated in the July Monarchy, but Tocqueville's correspondence shows that he was already thinking along these lines.

Democratic Ideologies. Nineteenth-century French democrats were, more often than not, republicans who looked for inspiration to the great revolution. Or rather, they looked back with special excitement to *their* part of the revolution, the years from 1792 to 1794. This democratic or republican ideology had a religious intensity inspired by a few main themes: popular sovereignty, nationalism, a vigorous foreign policy, liberation of other peoples from foreign and upper-class control, anticlericalism, the secular state, and progress through science and education. Romanticism and growing historical awareness gave emotional power to these associations. For some, the insurrections which failed to unseat Louis Philippe brought forth new martyrs.

This democratic ideology was not incompatible with liberalism, but clearly its substance was not the same as, for example, the democratic liberalism of Tocqueville. The growth of democratic ideology is not easy to measure. After the repressive September Laws of 1835, members of parliament no longer dared call themselves republicans, but referred to themselves as radicals or democrats. A newcomer (since 1841) to the Chamber, Ledru-Rollin (*see Reading No. 23*), rallied the radicals around his paper *La Réforme,* which first appeared in August, 1843. Jules Michelet, whose histories have already been mentioned, was a militant democrat and nationalist, a printer's son whose genius contributed powerfully to the *mystique* of the common people's emergence in history. The poet Alphonse de Lamartine, who came from a noble, royalist, Catholic family, at first refused to serve the July Monarchy but was elected to the Chamber in absentia in 1833 and became more and more democratic and personally popular as one of the parliamentary opponents of Guizot's regime. (*See Reading No. 19.*) The democratic and republican ideology was shared by many socialists such as Louis Blanc, although some socialists, for example, Fourier, were contemptuous of parliamentary reforms and ballots.

Socialist Ideologies. The word "ideologies" applies particularly well to socialism, which appeared in many isolated versions in the first half of the 19th century. Socialism—the word originally used in England and France in the 1830's—was usually not connected with political movements or labor organizations. In almost every case the socialists were intellectuals and moral critics, acquainted at most with a few disciples. In most cases they wished to persuade rather than to use force. Their common concern was to emphasize the cooperative and social rather than the competitive and individual. Their inspirations were similar: humanitarianism; very often religious feelings; faith in science and progress; the egalitarianism of the French revolution; hostility to economic liberalism; awareness of problems caused by industrialism.

After the apparent defeat of the Saint-Simonians and Fourierists in the early 1830's, socialism flourished again in the 1840's with great variety. It was this atmosphere of ferment which Karl Marx discovered in 1843 when he entered the exhilarating intellectual climate of Paris. Marx later called his predecessors "utopians" because he thought he had a better historical and scientific sense; but, in fact, he had been their pupil.

Pierre Joseph Proudhon was to rank with Saint-Simon and Fourier for originality and eventual influence. Proudhon was to live until 1865 and publish many books, but in the 1840's he was already making a name, and it may be said that his basic ideas were formed during the July Monarchy; this fact is sometimes offered in explanation of Proudhon's intense individualism which seems to reflect the society of peasant proprietors and artisans. Proudhon defended the freedom of the individual against economic exploitation, against the state, and against religion. He valued equality as well as liberty, and would sacrifice neither for the other. Proudhon, son of a barrel-maker and about as close to proletarian origins as any French socialist, was full of contradictions. His first famous slogan, "Property is theft," did not keep him from defending a society of small proprietors. He was, however, a consistent opponent of authority and the preacher of a doctrine of social cooperation by freely consenting individuals. He wanted workers to organize production and exchange, and interested individuals to organize other groups for other purposes. Society would be a federation of groups. Mutualism and federalism would do away with the wage system, the national state, and war. Parliamentary democracy could not make the state palatable to him. His tendency was toward anarchism.

To give some impression of the proliferation of writings by socialists or about labor problems in the 1840's, the following have been selected from more than 130 items from that decade listed by E. Dolléans and M. Crozier in *Movements ouvrier et socialiste* (Paris, 1950), pp. 40-48:

L'Atelier (Sept., 1840-Sept., 1850). A workingman's paper founded by workers. Influenced by Philippe Buchez's Christian socialism.

Blanc, Louis. *Organisation du travail* (1840). Very well-known book, well received by workers; author was journalist who used a phrase, "organization of labor" popularized by the Saint-Simonians; idea was for the state and philanthropists to provide workers of good character with funds so that they could set up their own workshops; Blanc believed in democracy and in a strong state; did not expect class warfare to result from organization of labor. *(See Reading No. 31.)*

Buret, Antoine Eugène. *De la misère des classes laborieuses en Angleterre et en France* . . . 2 vols. (1840). Like works of Villermé and Boyer, Buret shows concern about problems of labor. Buret's description antedated that of Engels. Buret recommended state intervention, e.g., use of taxation, to promote social reform.

Cabet, Étienne. *Voyages et aventures de lord William Carisdall en Icarie.* 2 vols. (1840).

————. *Comment je suis communiste et mon credo communiste* (1840). Imaginative utopian travel tale and statement of beliefs by lawyer who became public official and deputy. Cabet wanted democracy carried to extreme of community of belongings. He had an audience of workers as well as of intellectuals; one or two Icarian communities were tried in America without success. He favored setting an example rather than engaging in revolution.

Proudhon, Pierre Joseph. *Qu'est-ce que la propriété* . . . (1840) and various other works.

Villermé, Louis René. *Tableau de l'état physique et moral des ouvriers employés dans les manufactures de coton, de laine et de soie* (1840). Honest report; author optimistic despite horrors; the report attracted attention.

Boyer, Alphonse. *De l'état des ouvriers et de son amélioration par l'organization du travail* (1841).

Leroux, Pierre. *Discours sur la situation actuelle de la société et de l'esprit humain.* 2 vols. (1841). Former Saint-Simonian, author of many works, widely influential, he popularized the word "socialism" and preached a romantic synthesis of Christianity, democracy, and equality.

Buonarroti, Philippe. *Système politique et social des Egaux* (1842). The old conspirator, associate of Babeuf, continued to inspire revolutionaries.

Pecqueur, Constantin. *Théorie nouvelle de l'économie sociale et politique ou études sur l'organisation des sociétés* (1842). Former Saint-Simonian with ideas of economic interpretation and class struggle but also of democracy and Christian socialism.

Bonaparte, Louis Napoléon. *Extinction du paupérisme* (1844). The future Napoleon III had already published *Rêveries politiques* (1832) and *Des idées napoléoniennes* (1839), in which he claimed for Bonapartism a peculiar democratic virtue contrasting with the rather stuffy Orleans regime. (*See Reading No. 20.*) He wrote the book on pauperism while in prison and showed the influence of Louis Blanc and of the Saint-Simonians, advocating work projects and economic development on an imaginative scale.

Fourier, Charles. *Oeuvres complètes.* 6 vols. (1841-1846). Fourier had died in 1837. (See Considérant.)

Tristan, Flora. *Union ouvrière* (1843). Excellent example of how intelligent people were concerned about social questions. She is one of many lesser-known observers. (*See Reading No. 28.*)

Considérant, Victor. *Exposition abrégée du système phalanstérien de Fourier* (1845). Widely read popularizer of Fourierism.

Blanqui, Louis Auguste. (Included despite a paucity of authenticated publications. He spent the 1840's in prison.) An important revolutionist, noted for many attempts at violent revolution; spent 40 of his 79 years in various jails; became a legendary figure; one of the first professional revolutionaries; tried unsuccessfully to find a way by which an elite could take advantage of a revolutionary situation to seize power. His objective was a democratic and socialist republic.

Interest in the social question was also intensified by writers such as the novelist George Sand and the historian Michelet, by the example of Lamennais and by the social service work of the Catholic Society of Saint Vincent de Paul founded by Frédéric Ozanam and others. It is difficult to measure the effects on illiterate workers of this growing discussion, but their popular songs show that there were some effects.

Nationalism and Ideologies. French nationalism, the patriotism of the French to their nationality, their supreme loyalty to their nation, had become deeply involved with experiments in self-government. The French remained nationalistic under the Restoration and July Monarchy, but their leaders walked softly for fear of awakening the sleeping giant, the people. The traditionalists were wary as yet of nationalistic appeals, lest they trigger the reflex Fraternity-Equality, or Fraternity-Popular Sovereignty. Louis Philippe and the Orleanists gathered all the glories of France under their roof, including Napoleon's remains, but were concerned to make plain that they, and not a sovereign people, were the custodians. Democrats and republicans wanted France to stand for national self-determination in every sense, at home and abroad. Socialists in this period were of a similar bent, but there were already a few who opposed nationalism as inimical to the brotherhood of mankind.

Perhaps in Louis Philippe's time there was no full-fledged Bonapartism in the sense of an ideology with a program and a substantial clientele. Louis Napoleon was certainly trying to put together such a combination; he had available the Napoleonic legend; he was striving to suggest that his family was especially suited to be entrusted with the destinies of the French nation; he was holding out the twin lures of social reform and economic development. But the overriding appeals which were to serve Louis Napoleon after 1848—longing for order and fear of the unknown—were still, in milder form, serving Louis Philippe. The July Monarchy would have to fail before Bonapartism would get its second chance.

8

FOREIGN AFFAIRS

Between 1815 and 1848 France was a revisionist power, disapproving of the 1814-1815 settlements. Not yet defeated by anything but a great coalition, France was still regarded with uneasiness, especially after the July Revolution. Yet the July Monarchy proved to be surprisingly moderate in its foreign policy.

The July Revolution. The July Revolution was an affront to the 1814-1815 peace settlements and set an example which conservatives feared would be followed in the rest of Europe. For a time, with troubles spreading in Belgium, Poland, Italy, and Germany, no one could say where the 1830 revolutions would stop. Revolutionaries everywhere hoped that France would come to their aid. In France, leftists talked freely about a war in which peoples would be liberated and democratic ideas would spread. Laffitte and Lafayette and other leaders of the triumphant July Revolution shared the public excitement and made bellicose statements, but the king worked behind the scenes to minimize the effects of nationalistic fervor. He was a sincere moderate, and he knew that if France became too aggressive the coalition of 1815 would form again. But Louis Philippe did not favor peace at any price.

The Belgian Crisis. At the close of the Napoleonic wars Belgium had been joined to the Kingdom of the Netherlands as a barrier against France. Shortly after the July Revolution the Belgians declared their independence. Austria, Russia, and Prussia favored intervention, but Metternich hesitated to send troops which might be needed in Italy. Nicholas I of Russia said that he was prepared to send 60,000 men against the Belgians, but he preferred joint action with Austria and Prussia because of what France might do. There was also some doubt about Britain's position.

This was the time when the post-revolutionary effervescence in France was at its height. Public opinion favored aid to the Belgians. Louis Philippe could not afford to appear timid, but he wanted peace, and he knew that Britain would not stand for French annexation of Belgium. On the other hand, he could not afford to let any of the great powers crush so close a neighbor. Louis Philippe took a stand which he called "non-intervention," making it clear that France did not intend to stir up revolutions all over Europe, but would fight if anyone else intervened in matters which were closely related to French security. Sending the aged Talleyrand to London to negotiate with Wellington, Louis Philippe secured British support. Once it was clear that France was not trying to make a satellite of Belgium, the British Foreign Office was willing to support Belgian independence.

The Anglo-French entente was followed by international recognition of Belgium (December, 1830). Later, with British approval, Louis Philippe sent forces to help the Belgians resist a Dutch attack. Although criticized by the French for his caution, Louis Philippe refused the offer of the Belgian crown to his son, the Duke of Nemours; acceptance would have alienated the British. The Belgians chose Leopold of Saxe-Coburg, and as matters turned out, Louis Philippe's daughter Louise married Leopold and reigned as Belgian queen until her death in 1850.

Other Reverberations of 1830. Elsewhere in Europe Louis Philippe's policy of nonintervention meant that France would not crusade against the Vienna settlements. French and foreign liberals were disappointed; they wanted "nonintervention" to mean that France would protect other peoples from Austrian and Russian intervention.

In Poland, which was a Russian satellite kingdom, the French and Belgian examples and the readying of Polish troops by the Russians for possible use against Belgium had stimulated a nationalist rebellion in November, 1830. Nicholas I of Russia, after waiting upon events in central and western Europe, finally ordered a large army into

Poland (February, 1831). Despite a wave of popular emotion in Britain and France, no help was sent from the west. In London, Palmerston distrusted Polish independence as possibly shifting the balance of power toward France. In Paris the Chamber merely declared its sympathy for the Poles and the government sent a note urging the Russians to be moderate. Warsaw fell in September, 1831. Henceforth Polish exiles were to be a familiar part of the Parisian world of politicians and moralists from all lands.

In the Italian peninsula there were liberal revolts in Romagna, Modena, and Parma. Metternich's Austria sent troops. The new French government agreed not to act, provided the Austrians would withdraw as soon as order was restored. In 1832, however, after Austrian troops had re-entered the peninsula, the energetic Casimir Perier sent a French force to occupy Ancona on the Adriatic coast.

In the German Confederation, as in Italy, liberal revolts worried Metternich, whose preoccupation with Central Europe helps explain the success of Louis Philippe's diplomacy. The Habsburgs, Hohenzollerns, and Romanovs gave diplomatic recognition to Louis Philippe, but only because of their inability to overthrow him, and they never really accepted him as one of themselves.

The First Franco-British Entente. While Austrian, Prussian, and Russian diplomats met together at Münchengrätz in 1833 and reaffirmed the principle of intervention wherever jacobinism threatened the social order, the two western constitutional monarchies continued their cautious friendship. There was no formal alliance; the British told the French in 1833 that they wanted only treaties for specific purposes, and not general commitments. This was to be a British policy until the First World War. But for a time in spite of high French tariffs, commercial rivalries, and jumpiness over the balance of power in the Mediterranean, Britain and France were cordial to each other. The entente collapsed at the end of the 1830's, but was revived again for a time in the 1840's.

Colonial Problems. Although Napoleon lost most of France's colonies, many of them were recovered in the peace settlements of 1815: trading posts in India, for example, and way stations on the African coasts, and West

Indies islands. Mercantilistic economic policies returned with these colonies and were practiced in the Restoration and, without many changes, in the July Monarchy. Napoleon had abolished the slave trade, but slavery itself was not outlawed in the colonies during the July Monarchy. One of the reverberations of the Revolution of 1830 was a slave rebellion in the West Indies, which the French suppressed. Louis Philippe's government tried to enforce the prohibition of the slave trade, but abolition of slavery was postponed in spite of a report prepared by Alexis de Tocqueville.

The colonial policies of the July Monarchy were cautious because of the entente with Britain, because attention centered on domestic economic development, and because liberal economic theories worked against colonization. For the most part, private interests, especially those of merchants and missionaries, forced decisions on the government. The need for naval bases also played a part. French stations on the coast of Senegal and the Gulf of Guinea in Africa were extended. In 1836 the Jesuits were expelled from Tahiti on the initiative of the English trader-missionary Pritchard, but in 1838 a French naval squadron reversed this decision. The eventual expulsion of Pritchard led to a dispute with Britain in 1844 in which Guizot felt compelled to offer an indemnity to Pritchard and renounce annexation of the island, but France retained a protectorate. A French consulate in the Philippines was established in 1836 to aid commerce in the whole Far East. In 1839 the French made a commercial treaty with the indigenous government of the Hawaiian Islands. In the 1840's there was increased interest in the Pacific because of the prospect of trade with China, opened by the British in the Opium War of 1840-1842. The French secured similar trading rights in 1844. The route around Cape Horn was important enough to encourage the taking of bases in the Pacific between South America and China, but French efforts to colonize New Zealand were outpaced by the British. Guizot's policy after 1843 was to compromise by saying that France would not attempt to colonize large territories but would merely seek way stations useful to the navy and to commerce.

France's "second colonial empire" was for the most part

to be built after 1850. But there was one momentous beginning under the July Monarchy which was for over a century to have a special place in French history. This was the taking of Algeria.

Algeria. On the eve of the July Revolution Charles X's government had sought prestige through military victory and had succeeded in taking the city of Algiers. Nominally under Turkish rule, the large area which is now Algeria was then sparsely settled by Berbers and Arabs. The dey of Algiers was a local potentate who had long made trouble for Europeans through piracy and who prior to the French conquest had been engaging in a dispute with the French over commercial debts.

Louis Philippe had troubles enough at home and in Belgium and was, indeed, handicapped by having troops tied up in Algiers, and recalled some of them. The British were not pleased by the prospect of another French post on the Mediterranean. In general, French liberals had been hostile to Charles X's military project. On the other hand, now that the principal coastal city had been taken, Louis Philippe's new regime might lose face if this recent gain were too readily abandoned. Louis Philippe's policy was to hold on but do nothing rash.

Through most of the 1830's the French in Algeria tried to apply a policy of restricted occupation—the holding of coastal points together with enough of the interior to safeguard and provision them. Louis Philippe and the navy probably wanted to strengthen France's Mediterranean position but could not talk openly about Algeria, owing to the need for British friendship. Deputies in the Chamber became indignant at the financial costs and the occasional shocking bits of news, as when the French in 1836 were defeated in an effort to take the city of Constantine. Across the Mediterranean the French armies found themselves on the outskirts of a strange new world. (*See Reading No. 25.*) Veteran commanders found established routines inappropriate; young officers were fascinated and worked out new methods. From the beginning there were a few observers who said that the only way to make a success of the project was to occupy, colonize, and develop the whole country, but most people were poorly informed or hostile to the military and to imperialism.

Only from 1839 did the French begin to call the whole territory by one name, Algeria. The idea of unity was dramatized in that year by Louis Philippe's oldest son, the Duke of Orleans, who led a force from Constantine to Algiers, to prove that communication was possible. The trip was hazardous because for many years a gifted opponent, Abd el-Kader, had been trying to create an Arab state which would unite all the scattered tribes and drive the French infidels from the country. Throughout the 1830's the French forces were harassed and kept off balance as various generals failed to win security for their occupying forces. Constantine was taken in 1837 in a bloody assault in which Louis Philippe's second son, the Duke of Nemours, participated. But Abd el-Kader would not desist, and in 1839 he declared a holy war against the French.

The major steps in the conquest of Algeria were taken in the 1840's under General Thomas Robert Bugeaud, who was governor general from 1840 to 1847. (*See Reading No. 26.*) Although the French had briefly abandoned the policy of limited occupation in 1835, Bugeaud was the first official to get really massive military and financial support. Bugeaud had served in Napoleon's Imperial Guard, stayed out of politics under the Restoration, become a deputy in the July Monarchy, and led troops against the Paris insurrection of April, 1834. He was a tenacious, opinionated, and gifted commander, who knew how to care for troops and win their loyalty. Unpopular with the public for his conservative political views, he won the respect, though not the personal liking, of the able young "Africans," the French officers who had been serving in Algeria. Adopting some of their ideas, he practiced a war of movement coupled with devastation of Arab resources. It was a terrible war with atrocities committed on both sides.

Bugeaud wanted soldiers to be settled in Algeria as colonists, and this policy was tried on a small scale without much success. Others favored concessions to large capitalists. It was over such differences that Bugeaud resigned in 1847. Louis Philippe's son, the Duke of Aumale, who had served under Bugeaud, was then made governor of Algeria, and late in 1847 Abd el-Kader surrendered and was imprisoned in France. A substantial part of Algeria was now subdued; the European population had grown from about 7000 in 1833 to over 100,000. Pacification of the mountainous regions was to continue in the 1850's, and pacification of the Sahara was still taking place in the early 20th century.

The French advance in Algeria was a substantial piece of expansion at a time when Louis Philippe's foreign policy was otherwise very cautious. The British disapproved, but the slowness and vacillation of the French postponed friction. In 1844, however, the war had threatened to spread into Morocco. The Sultan of Morocco had been helping Abd el-Kader, Bugeaud had defeated the sultan's cavalry at the battle of Isly, and Louis Philippe's naval officer son, the Prince of Joinville, had bombarded the Moroccan ports of Tangier and Mogador. Louis Philippe, knowing that the British were alarmed by the spread of French influence toward Gibraltar, had made peace with the sultan, who had then ceased to provide a refuge for Abd el-Kader.

Spanish Questions. After the death of Ferdinand VII of Spain in 1833, the queen, Marie Christine, ruled as regent in the name of her daughter Isabella. This government had the support of Spanish liberals, but was opposed by the late king's brother, Don Carlos, who had conservative support. Civil war resulted. Britain and France favored Marie Christine, while Metternich favored Don Carlos, to whom he sent arms and subsidies. Louis Philippe concentrated troops near the Spanish frontier, and in 1834 made an agreement with Britain, which was intended to counteract the pressure of Austria, Prussia, and Russia, who favored Don Carlos and absolutism. In the same year, Britain and France made a similar agreement concerning Portugal, where a constitutional and an absolutist party were contending for power.

Despite this cooperation, the British and French were uneasy about each other's intentions in Spain. They supported rival wings of the Constitutionals, sought trade advantages for their respective countries, and could not help being aware of Spain's strategic importance, especially now that the French were in Algeria. With the defeat of the Carlists in 1839, the British secured economic advantages which irritated the French. By this time Britain and France had allowed their entente of the 1830's to lapse, and were opposing each other in the Egyptian crisis.

Spanish affairs of the 1840's aroused further hostility between Britain and France and helped bring to an end the renewed entente that they had patched together between 1841 and 1847. This time the source of friction was the affair of the "Spanish marriages." The young Spanish Queen Isabella might have married one of Louis Philippe's sons, had it not been for British opposition. Had it not been for French opposition, she might have married one of the eligible Coburgs related to Queen Victoria's husband, Prince Albert. In 1843 Louis Philippe and Queen Victoria agreed not to let their relatives compete for the hand of Isabella. Between 1844 and 1846, however, tricky maneuvers by both Palmerston and Guizot led to an open quarrel. Guizot arranged for the marriage of the Duke of Montpensier, Louis Philippe's youngest son, to the Spanish queen's sister, and also pressed for a simultaneous marriage of Queen Isabella to a cousin of hers who was not objectionable to the French. Palmerston claimed that France was trying to make a satellite out of Spain, and tried without success to renew a Coburg candidature for the queen's hand. Guizot's project won out. The Spanish marriages took place. The British were estranged from the French. Guizot probably hoped that Isabella would be childless, leaving the Spanish succession open to the Orleans family. If so, the queen soon disappointed him by giving birth to a son.

The Egyptian Crisis. The most serious diplomatic crisis of Louis Philippe's reign, next to the Belgian crisis, was the Egyptian affair of 1840. Egypt was well-known to the French from Napoleon's campaign and from French military, technical, and cultural influence there after 1815. Nominally a vassal of the Turkish sultan, Egypt's ruler, Mehemet Ali, had been in command since 1806. He had built up powerful military forces and supported the sultan against the revolution in Greece, but later sought to be an independent, hereditary ruler, expand Egypt, and possibly even take the sultan's place. No one knew how far Mehemet Ali would be able to go. He had been checked once, in 1833, after he had taken Syria, defeated the sultan's army, and prepared to march on Constantinople. On that occasion the Russians had reinforced the Turks. Britain and France had been glad to see the Ottoman Empire preserved, but unhappy about the increase in Russian influence. In 1839 the sultan's forces were again defeated after attempting to retake Syria, and again Constantinople was at the mercy of Mehemet Ali.

When people thought of the "Eastern question" they asked who would profit if the Ottoman Empire were partitioned, or ceased to be independent, or changed hands. Mehemet Ali's threat was alarming. If he were to revitalize the Ottoman Empire, both Russian influence and British trade might diminish. Mehemet Ali's advance in 1839 therefore revived the question of who would defend the sultan, and this time the British were first to do so, while the Russians remained passive, owing to internal problems. Even French policy was opposed to a move to Constantinople on Mehemet Ali's part; the French government had been aiding Egypt as a means of countering British supremacy in the Mediterranean, and as insurance for Algeria, but the French had no desire to gamble on the collapse of the Ottoman Empire or its transfer to Mehemet Ali. The French were willing, however, to see Mehemet Ali independent and possessed of Syria. The British, for their part, were appalled at the idea that French influence might one day extend from Algeria all the way around the Mediterranean to Syria.

The crisis came in 1840. Palmerston, impatient with the French, secured agreement of Austria, Prussia, and Russia to a settlement limiting Mehemet Ali to hereditary possession of Egypt, and some of Syria for life, but making him disgorge other gains. Mehemet Ali, relying on French support, rejected their ultimatum. A surge of French nationalism made it difficult for Louis Philippe to repudiate France's client in the face of the same coalition that had defeated Napoleon. The king allowed Thiers to trade bellicose statements with the Germans, in whom memories of Napoleon's last years evoked passionate anti-French feelings. But when British forces helped the Turks chase Mehemet Ali from Syria, the French did nothing. Louis Philippe, and doubtless Thiers, had no intention of engaging in a general war. France accepted the settlement arranged by the great powers. Thiers resigned, and Guizot was recalled from London to complete France's part in the international arrangements. France joined the other powers in signing the Straits Convention of 1841, which closed the Bosporus and Dardanelles to foreign warships in time of peace.

Failure of the Second Franco-British Entente. The second period of Franco-British friendship was made possible by the coming to power of a Conservative government in London, and by the good relations which Guizot enjoyed with Lord Aberdeen, who in 1841 succeeded Palmerston at the Foreign Office. In September, 1843, the young Queen Victoria, with her consort Prince Albert, visited Louis Philippe and his family in Normandy. Louis Philippe visited England in late 1844. He especially valued this English connection because the rest of European royalty refused to forget the barricades of 1830. Queen Victoria visited the Orleans family again in 1845.

It was difficult, however, to preserve amicable relations. In 1843 the British opposed a projected tariff union between France and Belgium. In 1844, between the first two royal visits, occurred the Pritchard affair, dramatizing Anglo-French competition in remote parts of the world. Palmerston's return as Foreign Secretary in 1846 contributed to the aggressive rivalry which characterized the Spanish marriages affair in its final stages. On the French side, Louis Philippe and Guizot tired of being criticized for subservience to Britain. British diplomacy, uneasy over French advances on the southern Mediterranean shore, worked against the French in Tunisia. British industrialists waited in vain for a lowering of French tariffs. Public acknowledgement that the Franco-British entente was ended came early in 1847.

The Eve of 1848. In 1847 Guizot and Metternich exchanged views and seemed to be preparing a Franco-Austrian entente. Such an outcome would have been in keeping with Louis Philippe's encouragement of peace and order. Metternich lacked confidence, however, in the stability of Louis Philippe's regime, while Louis Philippe and Guizot, for their part, could not afford to cooperate too readily with the victor of 1815.

Late in 1847 international alignments were tested by a brief civil war in Switzerland, in which the league of Catholic cantons, the *Sonderbund,* was defeated by the forces of the Federal Diet. Metternich favored the more conservative *Sonderbund.* Britain favored the Diet, which stood for reform of the Swiss constitution. Here was an opportunity for France to line up with Austria and checkmate Britain. Louis Philippe and Guizot did not do so, but neither did they take the liberal side.

As the year 1848 opened, there were signs of unrest in the Italian and German states as well as in France. Metternich was increasingly pessimistic. Frederick William IV of Prussia was toying with a united diet. From London Palmerston was encouraging continental liberals and advocating liberal reforms. In France Louis Philippe and Guizot were under fire from such leaders as Lamartine and Thiers for having a reactionary foreign policy and were being attacked in the banquet campaign for the stodginess of their domestic policies. (*See Reading No. 32.*) The July Monarchy had stood for peace and had denied to revolutionary movements the inspiration of French support. The February Revolution in Paris removed this restraint, and for a moment anything seemed possible in Europe.

9

LOUIS PHILIPPE AND GUIZOT

In 1840 Louis Philippe, at the age of 67, was entering the long period of political stability which was to be associated with the ministry of Guizot. Neither of the two men foresaw the length and closeness of their collaboration. Guizot's appointment suited Louis Philippe's need to reverse the belligerent foreign policy of Thiers and to reassert the royal authority. Guizot stood for peace and shared Louis Philippe's conception of a first minister as a man with whom the king should be able to collaborate. The aging king, remarkably knowledgeable but no longer keeping up with the aspirations of the century, and the stern minister whom the songwriter Béranger described as having the head of a poet and the style of a geometer, found each other unexpectedly congenial. The formal head of the ministry was Soult, who held this position until his retirement in September, 1847. Guizot, the real head, was also Minister of Foreign Affairs.

The Royal Family. The Orleans family at the start of the 1840's had lost one of its members, Marie Christine, Duchess of Württemberg, who had died the year before. The other daughters were Louise, Queen of Belgium, who was now 28, and Clementine, Princess of Saxe-Coburg, who was 23. Their brother, the heir to the throne, was Ferdinand Philippe, Duke of Orleans, now 30, an independent, active young man, veteran of the Algerian war. He was married to a German princess, Helen of Mecklenburg, and had two sons, one of them two years of age, the other newly born. The whole family was proud of Ferdinand Philippe, and he was expected to be a vigorous, liberal monarch when his turn came.

Louis Philippe's second son, the Duke of Nemours, was 26. Reputed to be his father's favorite, he was a thin, sober, blond young man, with a reputation for conserva-

tism. Joinville, the third son, was a naval officer of 22.
The fourth and fifth sons, Aumale and Montpensier, were
18 and 16, respectively. Aumale, upon his return from
service in Algeria in 1841, was fired upon while parading
with his brothers in the Faubourg Saint-Antoine. The bullet
struck a nearby officer's horse in the eye, killing it instantly.
The would-be assassin was captured and found to be a
member of a secret society, the Egalitarians. He was sentenced to death, but Louis Philippe commuted the sentence.
The king himself was shot at twice in 1846, by mentally
disturbed persons.

In the royal household the queen, Marie Amelia, continued to be devout, unassuming, devoted to her family and
to charities, a person of natural dignity, and a source of
strength to all. The king's sister, Madame Adelaide, died
on December 31, 1847—a severe blow to the old king.
Opinions differ as to whether she had been urging him
to be less inflexible politically.

Louis Philippe continued to be kindly, affable, even-
tempered, and remarkably enduring in his physical and
mental powers. Toward the end of his reign when difficulties were accumulating, he showed occasional signs
of nervousness and irritability, but these were exceptions.
The principal weakness of his age was increasing inflexi-
bility; he was strong in continuing the routine, but less
able to change it. He was also inclined to overestimate his
own and his family's popularity.

Despite their loyalty to each other, the members of the
Orleans family were not always in harmony. The heir to
the throne was generally considered to be more liberal
than his father, and a partisan of a more vigorous foreign
policy. Toward the end of the reign, Louise, Queen of the
Belgians, expressed privately her concern over her father's
political posture. Joinville and Aumale were also critical,
and this fact may account in part for their being away on
military service in the crucial February days of 1848.
During these last days Louis Philippe's large and loyal
family was unable to help him. These circumstances
might have been different but for an unfortunate accident
in 1842.

The Death of the Heir. On July 13, 1842, the heir
to the throne, the Duke of Orleans, died of injuries re-

ceived in falling from a carriage pulled by a runaway horse. The event was a terrible blow to the Orleans family and to the July Monarchy. The heir to the throne died at 32. Although known to be impatient with the sluggishness of the regime, he had been tactful enough to keep out of politics and devote most of his time to the army. Louis Philippe was in his seventieth year at the time of his son's death. Now suddenly the new heir to the throne was a boy of four. (*See Reading No. 24.*)

After a funeral at Notre Dame, witnessed by thousands, Louis Philippe faced the sad task of providing a regency for his grandson. Should a constitutional provision be written, or was it enough to provide for this one case by choosing between the boy's mother and his uncle, the Duke of Nemours? For a moment the abyss which had been glimpsed in 1830 was briefly present as the Radical Ledru-Rollin proposed that the nation be consulted. But the men of July closed ranks. Guizot said that the king and the two chambers, "the only legitimate and regular organs of the national sovereignty," should make the decision. Thiers came to Guizot's aid. There was still division of opinion concerning whether the parliament should support the widow or the uncle, the one thought to be liberal, the other conservative, but the king and Guizot had their way and Nemours was approved by both chambers.

The Pretenders. The Legitimist pretender to the throne was the Duke of Bordeaux, born after his father's assassination in 1820. Since the Duchess of Berry's attempted insurrection in 1832, there had been confusion in Legitimist ranks. *"Emigrés* in their own country and their own century," the Legitimists excelled in ridicule of Louis Philippe's monarchy, but were divided on tactics—for example, extension of the suffrage—and plagued by personal rivalries. After Charles X's death at Gorizia in northern Italy in 1836 his oldest son, the Duke of Angoulême, took the title of Louis XIX. Inside France, however, the Duke of Bordeaux was recognized by most Legitimists as Henry V.

In 1843 the Duke of Bordeaux took a public position as pretender. Journeying to London as the Count of Chambord (a title by which he was to be known for the rest of his life), he held a reception at Belgrave Square. Many Frenchmen attended, including Chateaubriand, and for a time Louis Philippe was worried lest Queen Victoria recognize the pretender, but this was the year of the queen's visit to France, and the *entente cordiale* held. The pilgrimage of Legitimist deputies to Belgrave Square led to stormy recriminations in the French parliament.

In May, 1846, Louis Napoleon, the Bonapartist pretender, escaped from fortress imprisonment at Ham, where he had for six years been reading (he called it the "University of Ham"), corresponding (with Louis Blanc, for example), and writing (*The Extinction of Poverty*, 1844). The French government had been willing to release him on condition that he abandon his claim to the imperial throne, but he had refused. In truth, Louis Philippe was not much concerned about the little adventurer; the Legitimists and republicans worried the king, but Bonapartism seemed dead. Louis Napoleon made his way to London to await another turn of the wheel of fortune.

Parliament. Parliament during the Guizot years was not influenced very much by the changing life of the country. True, the very limited electorate grew with the general prosperity, but it remained small enough to be watched over with ease. Guizot systematically harvested the votes of government jobholders and made certain that other voters knew his wishes. In the era of railroad building there were close relations between political loyalty and patronage. Within the Chamber Guizot strengthened his majority, making full use of deputy functionaries. Protests multiplied against the double role of these men; there were seven debates on this question between 1841 and 1847. Parliamentary and electoral reforms (i.e., an end to deputy functionaries, and an extension of the suffrage) were demanded with vigor in 1842 and in 1845-1846. In 1842 and 1846, after his majority had rejected these demands, Guizot dissolved the Chamber and held new elections, which strengthened his position.

The historic Guizot ministry was really a "Right" or "Resistance" ministry supported by a majority made up of Conservatives from the Center and Right of the Chamber. There were a few Legitimists to the right of Guizot's majority, but the principal parliamentary opposition came from the Left-Center and Left of the "dynastic" (loyal to the monarchy) deputies, led by Thiers and Odilon

Barrot. Thiers' Left-Center and Barrot's Dynastic Left frequently cooperated in demanding parliamentary and electoral reforms of a moderate nature, but fortunately for Guizot they disagreed on other issues, for example, the regency question in 1842.

The extreme Left of the Chamber consisted of republicans (as distinguished from Barrot's Dynastic Left). To avoid prosecution they called themselves "Democrats" or "Radicals." They were numerically weak in the Chamber and, indeed, outside of it as well, but unlike the other parliamentary groups they had a measure of organization and a fairly definite program. The leader of the Radicals in the Chamber was Alexandre Ledru-Rollin, who was elected in 1841 following the death of the esteemed Etienne Garnier-Pagès. Ledru-Rollin's statements as a candidate were so radical that he was prosecuted by the government and only escaped punishment after an appeal and a retrial. His program, expressed in his campaign speeches (*see Reading No. 23*) and in the newspaper *La Réforme*, started in 1843, celebrated popular sovereignty and aimed at universal suffrage and social reform. Some of the shareholders of this paper were Etienne Arago, Louis Blanc, Godefroy Cavaignac, and Pierre Leroux, men with an eye to social as well as political problems. Those Radicals who gave priority to political objections tended to group themselves around a more moderate republican paper, *Le National*. A good many Radicals, discouraged by the apparent stability of the regime in the 1840's, would have been satisfied by moderate steps in the direction of a democratic monarchy. On the other hand, the Radicals in parliament, respectable, well-to-do reformers, were linked by chains of acquaintances to obscure, potentially violent men, republican practitioners of insurrection, whom they did not know personally but who were part of the revolutionary tradition looking back to 1793.

Lamartine, the romantic poet who was elected to the Chamber in 1833, was making his way toward the left without committing himself to any party. In 1839 he issued a celebrated warning. (*See Reading No. 19*.) Alexis de Tocqueville was also a deputy in the 1840's. He was not an orator or an organizer of men. His parliamentary activity after his election in 1839 was most effective in committees

devoted to specific problems: slavery, colonial problems,
prison reform. In his opinion the *pays légal* and Guizot's
parliament were impermanent because they did not represent sufficiently the life of the nation. Tocqueville's career
in the Chamber was climaxed by a remarkable speech on
January 27, 1848, in which he warned of the dangers which
were to appear in the February revolution a month later.
(*See Reading No. 33.*)

Ministerial Responsibility. Guizot's long ministry was
at all times responsible to the parliament, and was a step
in the direction of parliamentary government; yet it falsified the principle of responsibility by pressure on electors
and deputies, and by staying in power so long with the help
of such devices, it contributed to the explosion which
turned France away from parliamentary government for
a generation.

To be sure, pressure from above in elections and on
parliaments had not been unknown in Britain, and as
Guizot said, the British crown retained considerable influence. (*See Reading No. 29.*) Nevertheless, a "palace
party" looked vulgar and old-fashioned by the 1840's
and in addition there was in Guizot's version of parliamentary government a potential hazard which the British
had escaped at the end of the 18th century. At a time
when the principle of political responsibility of ministers
was being learned, it was dangerous and confusing for a
legally inviolable monarch to identify himself too closely
with ministers whom the parliament was supposed to watch
and criticize.

The imperfections of Guizot's long ministry certainly
contributed to the collapse of 1848. Yet, one is obliged
to consider how close France came to the lasting practice
of parliamentary institutions and how close Louis Philippe
and Guizot came to success. As the history of the Second
Republic was to demonstrate, the majority of the French
were not radical. They were, at most, uninspired by the
program of social conservatism, pacific foreign relations,
and dynastic ambition pursued by Louis Philippe and
Guizot. Although opposed to this program and much
stronger among the elites of youth and talent than in the
parliament, the democratic and social reform impulses were
not all committed to revolution. As for the Catholic and

Legitimist aristocracy with its remaining rural clienteles, it was more tolerant of the regime's conservatism than of its own heretical offshoots. Even the embryonic labor and socialist movements were still, in that springtime of innocence before the bloody June days of 1848, largely pacific and hopeful. True, these various tendencies pulled in different directions, but given time and the avoidance of another costly test of strength and doctrinal loyalties some second best program of least divisiveness might have withstood the stresses of the late 1840's.

Any such "solution" would have needed political expression through the parliamentary system. In the given circumstances an alternation in power of governments led by, let us say, Guizot and Thiers (Center and Right, Center and Left) might have made little difference in any one year. But if two such combinations had competed with each other sufficiently to introduce changes piecemeal into the political and social system, the rigidities of Louis Philippe's and Guizot's rule might have been altered and revolution avoided. Instead, the rigidities remained so long that an inoffensive protest against them, coming at an inopportune moment, unleashed forces which a mere shift from Guizot to Thiers was unable to contain.

Legislation. There was little legislation during the long Guizot ministry. France's first protective labor law (1841) was inapplicable to most workers (see p. 60). Guizot continued the building of fortifications around Paris begun during the Egyptian crisis of 1840. Tariff legislation was frequently debated, and there were many small changes in the various tariffs and prohibitions, but on the whole the high protective tariffs of the Restoration were altered very little. In academic circles there were economic liberals —Jean Baptiste Say, Pellegrini Rossi, Michel Chevalier, and Frédéric Bastiat—but most of the deputies were protectionist and preferred the arguments of Thiers and a number of "national economic" writers who gave priority to the nation's need to increase productivity while maintaining as much autonomy in economic matters as possible.

Much of the deputies' time was spent on concessions and permits to particular business enterprises and on noncontroversial legislation concerning road building (the mileage of major roads was doubled in the July Monarchy),

bridge building, canal digging, river dredging, and, after
1845, replacing the old semaphore system with electric
telegraph lines. Subsidies were paid to shipbuilders after
1841, and the state actually put into operation some
shipping lines of its own, including the LeHavre-New York
line begun in 1840. The state also ran a postal service.
The most spectacular innovation of the era was railroad
building, but there were years of delay, and France fell
behind the other major countries before a law of 1842
finally struck a workable formula. The state did much to
assume risks and assure profits to private capitalists (see
p. 56).

Church and Schools. In 1844 and again in 1847 the
government proposed projects which would have allowed
Catholics to have their own secondary schools, subject to
minimal state controls. Neither project was passed; one
died in the Peers, the other in the Chamber.

The July Monarchy was not hostile to the Church. After
the first year or so, the new regime welcomed support of
the Church against both the Legitimists and the extremists
of the Left. Pope Gregory XVI recommended submission
to Louis Philippe's government, and Catholics in general
favored the regime after it was clear that it was not anticlerical. Catholic laymen gave substantial gifts to the
Church. The Jesuits, who had 12 establishments in France
in 1828, had 74 in 1840. Catholics, well-treated by Guizot's
education law of 1833, which pertained to elementary
schools, were anxious to have their own secondary schools
without state control.

The Catholic campaign, which perhaps reached its
height in 1844, was conducted on many levels, from the
common touch and abusive genius of the journalist Louis
Veuillot, who made his debut at this time, to the eloquent
liberalism of the Catholic layman, Charles de Montalembert, who appealed for individual rights and free competition. Guizot recognized that there was a "liberal" issue
concerning the right of parents to educate their children in
schools not devoid of Catholic influence. On the other
hand, chords of nationalism and faith in progress were
touched by Victor Cousin's protest that if all religions had
their own schools the nation's youth would grow up in
fragmented groups, and by Michelet's and Quinet's attacks

on the Jesuits in their lectures at the College de France in 1843. The public was aroused more by the attacks on the Jesuits than by questions of liberalism and education. In the end, both sides were disappointed. Louis Philippe and Guizot disliked the public commotion and did not press for other education laws. Guizot took steps to get the Pope to agree to the dispersal of the Jesuits, and in 1845 it was publicly announced that they were going to cease operations in France; in fact the Jesuits were slow to close their establishments and had not done so entirely by 1848. The Catholic campaign for "freedom to teach" had proved a disappointment to its sponsors, but the "Catholic party" was a force to be reckoned with in future elections and parliaments.

The Banquet Campaign. In the elections to the Chamber in August, 1846, Guizot won his most comfortable majority, 291 of his followers (there were 184 deputy functionaries) to 168 of the opposition of all parties. The regime and the ministry seemed to have reached a new high point of security. At the end of that summer, however, the good times which France had been enjoying since 1842 gave way to a depression which lasted through most of 1847. It was in part the old pattern of hard times in an economy still dominated by agriculture: poor harvests leading to high food prices and decreased sales of other commodities, such as textiles, with resulting unemployment and social unrest in the towns paralleled by wandering vagabonds and pillaging in the country. France was also caught in an international cyclical slump which, added to her own overinvestment in the preceding good years, made credit scarce and profits and stock market prices tumble. Railroad building virtually ceased, with disastrous results for metallurgy and related industries, and much unemployment. These complications continued even when good harvests eased food prices in the fall of 1847. Toward the end of the year general business recovery set in, but the alarm of the well-to-do and the unruliness of the lower classes were not at an end, and reached into the revolution of February, 1848.

All this, from the government's point of view, was a heavy burden, for tax returns fell and grain had to be purchased from Russia. The budget of this most complacent of ministries was unbalanced, and its critics multiplied. The government's foreign policy efforts, amounting to a rapprochement with Metternich and his allies, stirred up bitter criticism. In the summer of 1847 the regime lost much of its dignity by the trial and sentencing of two peers—one a general and former Minister of War, the other a former Minister of Public Works—on a charge of corruption. The regime's image suffered further from the scandals revealed by the case of another peer who had assassinated his wife. For the reading public a contrast was provided by a renewed and romantic interest in the glories of the recent past. Thiers, out of office, had been publishing his *History of the Consulate and Empire*, and in 1847 there appeared accounts of the great revolution by Louis Blanc, Michelet, and Lamartine.

It was in this atmosphere of increasing contrast between the contemptibly familiar government and the aspirations of the mid-century that the banquet campaign began. In March, 1847, electoral and parliamentary reform measures were introduced in the Chamber and defeated by the Guizot majority (*see Reading No. 30*), although this time some of the "progressive conservatives" associated with Tocqueville sided with the opposition. In the weeks that followed, there were more protests. One deputy achieved a brief celebrity for crying: "What have you done since 1840? Nothing! Nothing! Nothing!"

Inspired by methods such as those used in England by Cobden and the Anti-Corn Law League, the opposition leaders of the Left-Center, Dynastic Left, and Radicals decided to appeal to a wider public than the parliament. On July 9, 1847, they held a banquet for electors and reformist deputies, sang the *Marseillaise*, and listened to speeches comparing Guizot to Polignac. Dozens of other banquets followed in various parts of France, and exciting phrases were heard about national sovereignty, about a coming "revolution of contempt" (Lamartine), and even about the "organization of labor," as radicals such as Ledru-Rollin and socialist intellectuals such as Louis Blanc took part. (*See Reading No. 32.*)

The banquets were not intended to start a revolution, and they had not shown signs of doing so by the end of 1847. They had contributed to the atmosphere of disenchantment with the regime, but it is difficult to estimate their influence beyond the educated and politically conscious minority of the population. There would be no revolution unless something more concrete and dramatic attracted the attention of a wider public and tied together the political crisis, which was dividing those responsible for order, and the economic and social crisis, which was still encouraging disorder.

THE FEBRUARY REVOLUTION

By 1848 the narrow political regime of the July Monarchy was wanting in respect, but the people of France were not revolutionary in large numbers. There was no peasant *jacquerie* threatening dues-collecting landlords, as in 1789, no fear in the middle classes that an aristocracy of birth would entrench itself in an Estates General and maintain legal inequality; the *pays légal* was entrenched in political but not in civil inequality, and the banquet campaign had not excited mass protests against this political discrimination. As in 1789 and 1830 social discontents were made less bearable by economic dislocations, but no insistent wholesale alternative to existing social relations was available. The variety of middle-class life was greater than ever, shading off from the *grande bourgeoisie* to the still-numerous descendants of the *sans-culottes* of the great revolution. There were now the beginnings of a wage-earning proletariat whose lot was inspiring social critics. Paris could be as dangerous as in 1789 and 1830 if the law enforcement agencies were to become demoralized in the face of an aroused populace. For this reason the loss of respect for the regime, its isolation from the aspirations of the politically conscious, the apathy of most of the population, and the weakening effects of a feud within the citadel of political privilege increased the possibility of revolution—if not another 1789, at least an 1830.

The Next-to-last Parliamentary Drama. On December 27, 1847, the parliamentary session opened. In debates of January and February, 1848, the reformers tried to unseat Guizot's ministry. To Louis Philippe's annual message, they replied with indictments; the atmosphere grew heavy with moral condemnation through which flashed technical critiques of foreign policy and finances. It was widely believed that the ministry would fall, but for the moment Guizot was unshakeable. He and Louis Philippe, like their opponents, were living in an illusion of security. Both sides assumed that the debates were taking place within a firmly established parliamentary regime. Of the opposition some, like Tocqueville, sensed danger, but most thought that the stakes were ministerial portfolios and parliamentary and electoral reforms of a mild nature.

In January a little cloud appeared. Some National Guard officers of Radical persuasion proposed to organize another banquet, and sought the support of the deputies of the Dynastic Left. The latter refused, but when Guizot forbade (January 14) the holding of the banquet, the Dynastic Left joined the Radicals in protesting this decision. Guizot's majority held narrowly against his combined critics. The Left-Center, Dynastic Left, and Radicals, unsuccessful in the Chamber, wanted to appeal to a wider public and therefore went ahead with plans for the banquet which Guizot had forbidden.

The End of the Banquet Campaign. This banquet differed from its predecessors in that it entailed a popular protest march to the banquet hall, to prove that Guizot's majority did not reflect the opinions of the massed students, National Guards, and workers. The marchers would meet in front of the Madeleine church on February 22 at ten in the morning and would accompany the banqueters to their destination. Peaceful pressure was the intent, but pressure enough, it was hoped, to worry the king and break the resolution of Guizot's majority. Violence and revolution were not contemplated; even the republicans remembered how Louis Philippe had dominated every insurrection; they did not mean to give the government any excuse to repress them.

After these resolutions came misgivings. Paris was not the safest place in Europe for moderates to encourage a demonstration. This thought crossed the minds of both the moderate opposition and the government authorities, and a truce was arranged. The banqueters would find police in the dining room, would protest formally, and would take the case to court.

But this caution came too late. The less moderate oppositionists considered the public procession to be more essential than the banquet. The procession, they felt, must go on. Without consideration for the compromise arranged by their hesitant brothers, these radicals on February 21 published directions for the protest march on the following day.

The government at this point prohibited any public demonstration. A political committee, it was argued, had no authority to call out the National Guard and the students. It was against the law to hold a public gathering without a permit. This action was discussed in the Chamber, but even the opposition had to admit the correctness of the government's stand. So the opposition deputies, backing down, abandoned both the procession and the banquet and switched to the face-saving device of indicting the ministry for blocking the banquet in the first place. Steps were taken to head off the local organizers of the procession, lest the government be given a pretext for crushing the democratic movement. This unwinding process was not going to be easy if neighborhood leaders refused to cooperate. The police were warned that there might be some scattered fights, but the government expected no insurrection.

Tuesday, February 22. On this rainy morning by nine o'clock crowds were circulating in front of the Madeleine and in the nearby Place de la Concorde. On the Left Bank, in the Latin Quarter, after a night of debates and speeches, students assembled at the Panthéon and moved by way of the boulevards Saint-Michel and Saint-Germain toward the center of the city, paying a disrespectful visit to the Palais Bourbon on the way. There was shouting, singing, and some throwing of stones, but the day passed without a crisis. The leaders of secret societies of radicals and armed workers held back and watched the spontaneous demonstrations with speculative eyes. In the Chamber, seated in the Palais Bourbon across the river from the Place de la Concorde, a petition accusing the ministry was presented by the leader of the Dynastic Left, Barrot. That evening crowds made bonfires of chairs from the cafés along the Champs Elysées and skirmished with the troops sent to disperse them. There were signs that veteran street fighters were active. Here and there gunshops were ransacked. Scattered barricades went up in the poorer neighborhoods. Public buildings were attacked. In reply the government sent regular troops to prearranged stations and called out National Guard units. By midnight there was a deceptive air of calm. Neither the full ingenuity of radical neighborhood chiefs nor the loyalty of the government's defenders—and particularly that of the National Guard—had been fully tested. Guizot thought the worst was over. At the Tuileries Palace, Louis Philippe read the reports with satisfaction. He had known worse days. But in fact the manifestation begun by moderate reformers was out of control and the night was alive with subversion.

Wednesday, February 23. It was still raining, but crowds of curious turned out. There were more barricades. Regular troops took their stations again, clearing some of the barricades on their way, but mainly they avoided clashes. The National Guard was counted on to keep order with a minimum of coercion. But the National Guardsmen as they assembled gave many indications that they were not marching through the dampness for Guizot's sake. There were cries of *"Vive la réforme"* and *"À bas Guizot."* Many Guard legions fraternized with the disorderly street crowds, and some took their side against regular troops and police. The National Guard had been the July Monarchy's right arm since 1830, but on this day its appearance in the streets made matters worse. Louis Philippe had taken this bourgeois military force too much for granted; he had not held a full-scale review since 1840. Now it was evident that most of the officers sympathized with the Dynastic Left's opposition, while many of the rank and file were Radicals.

The behavior of the National Guard was a devastating fact which burst in upon Louis Philippe's complacency. Evidently if he wanted his way he would have to subdue the citizen soldiers upon whom he had most depended. In the early afternoon, heeding the advice of the General Staff and the entreaties of the queen, Louis Philippe dismissed Guizot. At the Palais Bourbon Guizot's majority learned from their master himself that he had fallen before the extra-parliamentary pressure of the National Guard.

To rally the National Guard to a reform program, and restore order in the city, the most likely replacement was Thiers, leader of the Left-Center, or even Barrot, of the

Dynastic Left. But Louis Philippe distrusted Thiers, the critic of his foreign policy, the orator of "reign, not rule." The king wanted his old standby, Molé, who in the eyes of the public and the parliament was no better than Guizot. Molé appeared at the Tuileries at four in the afternoon and tried to decline the honor, in part because Thiers refused to serve in his cabinet. Afternoon lengthened into evening and precious time was lost as Molé tried to form a government.

Through the city there was joyful disorder, with crowds still in the streets and the victorious National Guardsmen slouching homeward as the lights went on. Regular troops were still on guard, but no determined hand safeguarded public order. Police stations were broken into here and there, and prisoners released. Paris was ripe for an incident. At the Ministry of Foreign Affairs, Guizot's headquarters on the Boulevard des Capucines, there had been continuous tumult. Shortly after nine at night, a roving band confronted the regular troops on guard there and pressed them back as they tried to fix bayonets. Someone fired, and then a volley felled 50 or more people. The crowd recoiled in panic and then rallied as the frightened troops dispersed. The insurrectionists piled their dead into a wagon and paraded by torchlight through the center of the city.

Molé, at the Tuileries, learned the news and resigned. Louis Philippe named Thiers, and agreed reluctantly that Barrot should also take part in the Cabinet. Pressed by his advisors, the king named as commander of the armed forces General Bugeaud, the tough, unpopular conqueror of Algeria and of the 1834 Paris insurrection. But indignant crowds were arming themselves now in all parts of the city. The mood of celebration had changed to one of anger. More barricades were going up, and the National Guards were passing over to the insurrection.

Thursday, February 24. To win the city back from the insurrection, control the major streets—that was Bugeaud's problem as February 24 dawned cold and rainy. At six in the morning, he had four columns of regular troops on their way outward from the central fortress which the Tuileries Palace had become. Three were to clear their way through the barricades until they rescued the demoralized detachments isolated at the City Hall,

Place de la Bastille, and Panthéon. A fourth was to circulate and keep the most important passages open. Everywhere the troops were to announce the Thiers-Barrot ministry, in the hope of pacifying the crowds.

It is difficult to say whether this policy would have succeeded, for after an hour or so it was abandoned. General Bedeau's column was swinging in a big clockwise circle along the boulevards toward the Place de la Bastille when it was stopped by a barricade at the Boulevard Bonne Nouvelle. Bedeau hesitated, talked with the insurrectionist leaders, and was convinced that bloodshed could be avoided if news of the Thiers-Barrot ministry could be given time to spread. He sent for instructions to Bugeaud, the commander in chief. Bugeaud had all this time been under pressure from Louis Philippe's entourage to avoid bloodshed. Many of the king's advisors were pressing him to substitute the National Guard for the regular army. The upshot was that Bugeaud's columns were recalled to the Tuileries with orders to avoid firing on the people, and it was announced that the National Guard, not the regular army, would keep order as the new Thiers-Barrot ministry took office. This maneuver signaled the disintegration of the already shaky morale of the regular troops, while the National Guard did nothing to take their place. Vainly, Thiers sent the supposedly popular Barrot into the streets and persuaded Louis Philippe to agree to the dissolution of the Chamber and to new elections; these concessions went unnoticed by the turbulent crowds. But dissolution of the regular army units was placing the Tuileries in danger.

Toward noon Louis Philippe, looking out of his window at the remaining National Guard legions and regular troops in the courtyard of the Tuileries, had to decide whether to rely on these reserves or to leave Paris. To maintain their morale (and perhaps to test it), the old king went outdoors to review these troops, mounted on horseback and accompanied by his sons Nemours and Montpensier and by General Bugeaud and other officers, while Thiers and some of the civilians followed on foot. The procession made its way past the National Guard units first, to mixed cries of *"Vive le Roi!"* and, increasingly, *"Vive la Réforme!"* and *"À bas le système!"* Louis Philippe, without waiting for the response of the regular troops, turned his horse and re-entered the palace. Crowds began to infiltrate the great courtyard with its abandoned and leaderless army.

Inside the Tuileries final decisions had to be made. News was brought of further disorders, and amid confused bits of advice Louis Philippe tried a few last ineffective measures. Bugeaud and Thiers were replaced, in vain. The insurrection came closer. A short block from the Tuileries a frightful contest was occurring as a mob, unable to dislodge some desperate soldiers from a guard post, set fire to it and massacred the occupants. Soon the Tuileries would be invaded. Around Louis Philippe were the queen, their oldest and youngest living sons Nemours and Montpensier, their daughter-in-law the Duchess of Orleans with her son, the heir to the throne, and Marshal Soult, and other loyal retainers. The word "abdication" was spoken more and more openly, but the king and queen resisted, until finally, rewarded only with silence when he asked whether the Tuileries could be defended, Louis Philippe sat down and wrote out his abdication in favor of his grandson, the Count of Paris.

Flight was the next step. The palace was endangered on its northern side, near the Palais Royal, and there was some difficulty getting horses from the stables there. A groom was shot dead. Shortly after noon, Louis Philippe, the queen, Montpensier and his family, and several retainers left the Tuileries toward the Place de la Concorde and, escorted by some light cavalry, sped swiftly toward Saint-Cloud.

The Last Parliamentary Drama. It was still the noon hour of February 24, and there was still the problem of saving the Orleans monarchy. The Regent was Nemours. He was left behind in the Tuileries with his sister-in-law and the responsibility toward his ten-year-old nephew, who had just become king. Advice was plentiful and confused, but a decision had to come soon because armed bands from all over the city were converging by a natural instinct on the Tuileries. The Duchess of Orleans and her sons were taken to the Palais Bourbon, seat of the Chamber of Deputies, across the Seine from the Place de la Concorde. Nemours ordered the remaining troops in the Tuileries courtyard to retreat slowly to the Place de la Concorde to the west, there to join with other remaining troops in defense of the bridge leading to the Palais Bourbon. This retreat took place, and by about 1:30 in the afternoon the mobs were looting the Tuileries.

The last hope of the July Monarchy was that the parliament—the institution which had legitimized the regime in 1830—would stand by the dynasty, and that the troops outside the Palais Bourbon would stand by the parliament. At 1:30 the Duchess of Orleans and her children entered the Chamber and took seats. The deputies applauded. Nemours, the Regent, arrived shortly thereafter. The abdication of Louis Philippe, and the regency, were announced and applauded. But then a contest began with the republicans, who demanded that the duchess leave the session of the Chamber, and that a provisional government be formed. A debate ensued which became more and more confused and disorderly as armed insurgents forced their way into the hall. Barrot, leader of the Dynastic Left and prime minister designate since noon, defended the regency. Lamartine, in a dramatic speech, paid tribute to the courage of the Duchess of Orleans but supported the provisional government. More insurgents entered, unchecked by the troops outside the Palais Bourbon. (*See Reading No. 34.*) With difficulty, the Duchess of Orleans and her children were removed from the building. In the midst of disorder one of the republican factions—the moderate group associated with *Le National*—began proposing names for a provisional government. An appearance of legality was preserved by reading the list to the acclamations of the crowd. Shortly before four o'clock there was shouting that the City Hall was the place to form a government. Word had come that another republican faction, more radical, was taking control there. Part of the crowd swept out of the Palais Bourbon. They were followed shortly by the rest of the spectators and by the newly designated members of the provisional government, who made their way as best they could through the crowds on the riverbank to the City Hall, symbol of the Parisian and republican nature of the revolution.

By late afternoon and evening of February 24 the revolution was consummated. Insurrectionist leaders had taken over the Postoffice, the Prefecture of Police, and the city government, and linked together all of the forces on the barricades into one armed guard. At the City Hall a republican provisional government had been proclaimed before the massed crowds; in this tense situation the more moderate republicans of *Le National* had found it advisable to join to their list the names of the socialist Louis Blanc, the worker Albert, and others recommended by a committee from *La Réforme*, and by even more radical elements. The crowds choking the square outside the City Hall and roaming its corridors had been assured—in repeated proclamations with various amounts of qualification—that France was a republic.

— 11 —

THE FINAL EXILE

Flight to England. On the day of Louis Philippe's downfall, February 24, 1848, the king and queen and their party left Paris during the noon hour, passed by way of Saint-Cloud and Versailles, where the loyal General Dumas rented more carriages and horses, and then made their way toward the coast. The king and queen spent the night at their chateau at Dreux. The next morning they heard news of the failure of the regency and the proclamation of the republic. In disguise the king and queen made their way through the raw February weather to Trouville, near the mouth of the Seine, and after a period in hiding, they were conducted to an English ship at Le Havre. Masquerading as Mr. Smith, Louis Philippe spoke English. They landed in England on March 3. Meanwhile, after the failure of their efforts to establish a regency, the Duchess of Orleans went to Germany and the Duke of Nemours to England by way of Boulogne.

Last Years. Louis Philippe's last years were spent at Claremont house, a large, comfortable structure with its own park. The property was made available to him by his son-in-law, the King of the Belgians, to whom it had been granted by the British. The French provisional government permitted a few personal belongings to be sent to the exiled couple: silverware, books, a favorite carriage. The Orleans family's property was threatened with confiscation, but Thiers and others in the National Assembly succeeded in upholding the legality of Louis Philippe's transfer of this property to his children in 1830, although for a time it was sequestered pending a settlement of the family's debts. In 1852 Louis Napoleon was to decree the confiscation of much of this Orleans property and forbid members of the family to own real estate in France, but in the meantime Louis Philippe's last years saw him not unhappily absorbed in accounts and legal questions. His whole family gathered around him, for the revolution had cut short his sons' careers in the French services.

After the ordeal of the revolution and flight to England, Louis Philippe appeared aged, but he was still lucid and loquacious as ever. Guizot came to visit him, and in time so did Thiers. He was interviewed by journalists, and talked frankly and at length. He especially wished to defend his peaceful foreign policy. He also justified his abdication and passive departure from France. After the June Days of 1848 and the election of Louis Napoleon in December, Louis Philippe's record began to appear in a better light. The Orleans cause revived. There was also talk of a reconciliation between Orleanists and Legitimists. Louis Philippe never admitted to any incorrectness in his behavior in taking power in 1830, but he was willing to see a reconciliation of the two branches of the Bourbon family if it was possible. However, he left that problem for the next generation to solve.

Louis Philippe died in the midst of his family on the morning of August 26, 1850.

Part II

READINGS

— Reading No. 1 —

JOINVILLE'S RECOLLECTIONS OF THE 1830 REVOLUTION*

Louis Philippe's third son, the future Prince of Joinville, was 12 years of age in 1830.

✓ ✓ ✓

We went back to Neuilly in the evening, and the next day, the 26th, when Nemours and I were ready to leave for school, someone opened the door and shouted to our tutors: "The government 'coup' is in the *Moniteur*.—What?—Yes, the decrees." Hearing this our tutors ran to the family sitting room and we followed. We found my father sitting there like one prostrated; he was holding the *Moniteur*. When he saw the tutors, he raised his hand despairingly and let it fall again. After a period of silence during which my mother hastily told these tutors what had been happening, my father said only: "They are crazy!" Then, after a new and long silence: "They will have us exiled again. Oh! I have already been exiled twice! I don't want any more of it. I am staying in France!" . . .

. . . [Our] father disappeared from Neuilly. His movements were kept strictly hidden from us, and even since that time, I have never known much about them. So I shall say nothing about them.†

* [François], Prince de Joinville, *Vieux souvenirs, 1818-1848*. Paris, 1894, pp. 41-51, abridged.

† It is not for me to judge my father's accepting the crown in 1830. The July Revolution was doubtless a great misfortune: it struck a new blow at the monarchical principle and gave disastrous encouragement to speculators in insurrections. But I am absolutely certain that my father never wanted it, and that, on the contrary, he saw it happen with deep sorrow. When the throne of Charles X collapsed, without his being in any way able to protect it, he without any doubt wanted passionately to escape from the universal exile and continue to lead a happy life in France.

We merely knew after a short while that he was in Paris, that he was performing public duties as yet vaguely defined, and on the 31st, in the evening, my mother told us that we were going to rejoin him at the Palais Royal. About eight o'clock in the evening we set out, my mother, my aunt Adelaide and all the children, in an omnibus, in order not to attract attention. At the Étoile gateway we began to find some barricades, but they were already using openings to permit the passage of vehicles, all of the openings being guarded. . . . The omnibus could not go past Louis XV square because of the great number of obstacles. We got down and my mother, separating us two by two, told us to disperse and meet at the Palais Royal.

Paris was very curious, that evening: entirely illuminated, with lanterns and tricolored flags at each window. How had there been time in two days to make such a quantity of emblems? The streets were completely torn up and all the stones stacked for barricades, with a mixture of overturned vehicles, of barrels, of debris of every sort: behind all these barriers were improvised guards, passers-by, armed pedestrians firing their guns at each moment; everybody, men and women, with huge tricolored cockades in their hats, caps, bonnets, hair. On the square of the Palais Royal, one saw, in the midst of a great crowd, a stagecoach *Laffitte et Caillard,* which had been used in a barricade and then righted. It was full of people, overloaded with human clusters singing in chorus. Whenever the refrain stopped, a brisk fusillade was fired, and the stage coach, drawn by three or four hundred people attached to lines, made at great speed a tour of the square, in the midst of a concert of diversified howlings. Although it was late when we arrived at the Palais Royal, it was all lighted up, all the doors open; whoever wanted to came in, and when we climbed the staircase many people were already installed on the steps, preparing to spend the night there. We saw my father in his study and were sent to bed, that is, to bivouac in our usual rooms. . . .

. . . With the struggle ended and France up in arms from one border to the other, he understood that he would escape exile only by associating in the movement and it is certain that in the beginning he did so only with the thought of re-establishing Henry V on the throne. Once this hope was disappointed, he yielded to the entreaties of those who begged him, as the only one in a position to do so, to check France in its disastrous bent which would again lead it from republic to dictatorship, to invasion, to loss of strength. He was able to postpone for 18 years this deadly chain of events, at the cost of perpetual threats to his life. That will be to his honor in history, whatever may be the injustice of men.

— Reading No. 2 —

GENERAL DE RUMIGNY'S DIARY, JULY AND AUGUST, 1830 *

General de Rumigny had been a young officer under Napoleon. About 1818 de Rumigny became an aide-de-camp to Louis Philippe, whom he served loyally for 30 years. The dated parts of the general's diary were written from day to day and published long after his death.

✣   ✣   ✣

Paris, the 31st [*of July, 1830*]

. . . The Duke of Orleans sets out with the deputies for the City Hall. He goes on horseback, in the uniform of an officer general, and is surrounded by 100,000 men armed with all sorts of weapons; a single shot can be the end of him. I arrive right behind him at the City Hall, where a most extraordinary scene was awaiting us.

The crowd was so packed together that one could not force one's way through. The Duke of Orleans led the way, surrounded by men who cried: Look out! His horse was often carried along by the crowd who lifted it through passages in the barricades, and over holes made by the removal of paving stones. Poor Clio (the name of Monseigneur's mare) let herself be borne along like a lamb, without a single kick. . . .

As for me, I was on Pompée, a good grey animal, but separated from the others because I was never able to force my way through the crowd. M. Laffitte, in a sedan-chair, followed the Prince. The President of the Chamber also followed with at least a hundred deputies.

At the City Hall, the Prince was received by General Lafayette . . . and the Provisional Commission. The cheers of the populace were vigorous and stirring: Long live the Duke of Orleans! Long live liberty! Long live the Charter!

Faces were entranced; men and women of the people shouted and clapped in joy while throwing kisses to the Prince.

* Général Comte Marie-Théodore Gueilly de Rumigny, *Souvenirs* . . . Paris, Émile-Paul Frères, 1921, pp. 236-243, abridged. Reprinted by permission of the publishers.

"He has not betrayed us, nor abandoned us, not that one!!!"

The Prince mounted the stairs to the hall of columns in the City Hall. . . .

I was anxious, but the shouts of the crowd reassured me. Actually, in spite of their republican enthusiasm, they remained calm. . . .

The Prince appeared on the balcony of the great hall, holding General Lafayette by the hand. The shouts and applause then became frantic, and never has a prince been greeted with such joy by an armed populace. It was the rainbow after the storm.

This coming of the Duke of Orleans to the City Hall surprised Lafayette and the partisans of a republic. He put a good face on it and showed himself to be a good citizen. This moment determined the fate of the country.

The return of the Prince was as glorious as his arrival; however, burlesque was added to the grandeur, for, in front of Berthois and me at the head of the procession there was a man of the common people, almost naked, armed with a halberd from one of the Swiss guards at the Tuileries, who leaped and danced while twirling the halberd about and cleared the way by dint of rather frightening gestures. He accompanied us as far as the Palais Royal. . . . The populace hemmed in the Duke of Orleans with a barrier of loaded guns, held horizontally, crying: "Beware of the Jesuits." Absurd and ridiculous cries.

We arrived safe and sound at the Palais, where the Prince could consider himself lucky to be back, without any accident occurring to cast gloom over the general rejoicing. Never has a bolder or more decisive step been taken by a prince. . . .

August 2 [*1830*]

I have just summoned to the Palace, to guard it, a band of workmen commanded by two brothers: the Monsieurs de Vernon. To me, they look like robber chiefs; their men are in tatters. They were at the Bourse during the three days' fighting. They seized it. I asked Carbonet, aide-de-camp of General Lafayette, to let me have them, in a visit I paid him this morning.

With poorly armed laborers who are frightening in their really shocking getup, I am going to make a tougher police force than one made of the best soldiers in the world. Those men are the victors of the day!

I had one wretch stopped who wanted to proclaim a republic. My dear workmen gave him a thrashing with well-conditioned blows of the fist. If he had resisted, they would have torn him to pieces pitilessly.

In the courtyard of the Palais Royal, people sing the Marseillaise; boys from the schools persist in making violent remarks. If I were heeded, this opposition would not be allowed to grow, but General Lafayette is the protector of these trouble makers, and since they are all his friends from past conspiracies, we are obliged to tolerate outbursts which irritate me prodigiously.

— Reading No. 3 —

CHARLES X'S ABDICATION AUGUST 2, 1830*

My cousin, I am too profoundly pained at the evils which afflict or may threaten my people not to have sought a method of preventing them. I have therefore resolved to abdicate the crown in favor of my grandson, the Duke of Bordeaux.

The Dauphin, who shares my feelings, also renounces his rights in favor of his nephew.

You will have, therefore, in your capacity of Lieutenant General of the Kingdom, to cause to be proclaimed the accession of Henry V to the crown. You will in addition take all the measures which concern you in the matter of regulating the forms of the government during the minority of the new king. Here I confine myself to making known these arrangements; it is a means of avoiding further evils.

You will communicate my intentions to the diplomatic corps, and you will make known to me as soon as possible the proclamation by which my grandson will be recognized as king under the name Henry V.

I charge Lieutenant-General Viscount de Foissac-Latour to bring this letter to you. He has orders to come to an understanding with you about the arrangements to be taken in favor of the persons who have accompanied me, as well as about suitable arrangements for what concerns me and the remainder of my family.

We shall regulate afterward the other measures which are the consequences of the change of reign.

* J. B. Duvergier, *Collection complète des lois, décrets, ordonnances, règlements, et avis du Conseil d'État. . . .* Vol. 30, Paris, 1831, pp. 160-161.

I renew to you, my cousin, the assurance of the sentiments with which I am your affectionate cousin,

Signed, Charles Louis Antoine.

— Reading No. 4 —

DECLARATION OF THE CHAMBER OF DEPUTIES, AUGUST 7, 1830*

The Chamber of Deputies, taking into consideration the imperative necessity which results from the events of July 26, 27, 28, 29, and the days following and the general situation in which France is placed in consequence of the violation of the Constitutional Charter;

Considering besides that, as a result of this violation and of the heroic resistance of the citizens of Paris, His Majesty Charles X, His Royal Highness Louis Antoine, Dauphin, and all the members of the elder branch of the royal house are this moment leaving French territory;

Declares that the throne is vacant in fact and in law, and that it is indispensable to provide for it.

The Chamber of Deputies declares secondly that, in accordance with the will and in the interest of the French people, the preamble of the Constitutional Charter is suppressed, as wounding the national dignity in appearing to grant to Frenchmen rights which essentially belong to them, and that the following articles of the same Charter must be suppressed or modified in the manner to be indicated. . . .

On condition of the acceptance of these provisions and propositions, the Chamber of Deputies declares finally that the universal and pressing interest of the French people calls to the throne His Royal Highness Louis Philippe, Duke of Orleans, Lieutenant General of the Kingdom, and his descendants, in perpetuity, from male to male, by order of primogeniture to the perpetual exclusion of women and their descendants.

In consequence, His Royal Highness Louis Philippe d'Orleans, Lieutenant General of the Kingdom, shall be invited to accept

* Chambre des Députés; Session 1830; Impressions. Vol. I, No. 3, pp. 1-7, abridged.

and to swear to the clauses and engagements enunciated above, the observation of the Constitutional Charter and the modifications indicated; and after having done so before the assembled chambers, to take the title of King of the French.

Resolved at the palace of the Chamber of Deputies, August 7, 1830.

— Reading No. 5 —

THE CORONATION OF LOUIS PHILIPPE, AUGUST 9, 1830*

In the year 1830, on August 9, Messieurs the Peers and the Deputies, having assembled in the palace of the Chamber of Deputies, at the convocation of Louis Philippe, Duke of Orleans, Lieutenant General of the Kingdom, His Royal Highness entered, followed by Their Highnesses the Duke of Chartres and the Duke of Nemours and some officers of his household, and went to the position designated for him on the platform in front of the throne.

The Peers and Deputies stood, heads bare.

When His Royal Highness had taken a seat, he said to the Peers and Deputies: "Gentlemen, be seated."

Then addressing himself to the President of the Chamber of Deputies, he said:

"President of the Chamber of Deputies, will you please read the declaration of the Chamber."

The President did so, and then gave it to His Royal Highness, who delivered it to the provisional commissary in charge of the Department of the Interior.

Addressing himself also to the President of the Chamber of Peers, he said: "Will you please hand over to me the act of approval of the Chamber of Peers." This the President did, and he put the copy into the hands of Monseigneur, who entrusted it to the provisional commissary of the Department of Justice.

Monseigneur then read his acceptance, expressed thus:

* J. B. Duvergier, *op. cit.*, pp. 176-177.

"Peers and Deputies,

"I have carefully read the declaration of the Chamber of Deputies and the act of approval of the Chamber of Peers. I have pondered and considered all the terms.

"I accept, without restriction or reservation, the clauses and obligations included in this declaration, and the title King of the French which it bestows on me, and I am ready to observe it."

His Royal Highness then rose, and, head uncovered, took the oath, the text of which follows:

Oath.

"In the presence of God, I swear to observe faithfully the Constitutional Charter, with the modifications set forth in the declaration; to govern only by the laws and according to the laws; to have justice done to each according to his rights, and to act in all things uniquely for the interest, happiness and glory of the French people."

The provisional commissary in the Department of Justice next presented the pen to His Royal Highness, who signed the deed in three originals, for deposit in the royal archives and in those of the chambers of Peers and Deputies.

His Majesty Louis Philippe I, King of the French, then took his place on the throne, where he was hailed by shouts repeated a thousand times, "Long live the King."

When silence was re-established, His Majesty made the following speech:

"Peers and Deputies,

"I have just consummated a great deed. I feel deeply the extent of the duties it imposes upon me. I know that I will fulfill them. It is with this strong conviction that I have accepted the pact of alliance which was presented to me.

"I should strongly have preferred never to occupy the throne to which the national will has just called me: but France, its liberties attacked, saw that public order was in peril; the violation of the Charter had unsettled everything; the functioning of the laws had to be re-established, and it was the duty of the Chambers to attend to it. You have done it, Sirs; the wise modifications that we have just made in the Charter guarantee the security of the future; and France, I hope, will be happy at home and respected abroad, and peace in Europe strengthened more and more."

The provisional commissary in the Department of Justice then invited the Peers and Deputies to retire to their respective chambers, where the oaths of loyalty to the King, and of obedience to the Constitutional Charter and to the laws of the realm, were to be sworn to individually.

And the session was closed.

These minutes were drawn up and established at Paris, August 9, 1830.

Signed, Louis Philippe.

[*Other signatures*]

— Reading No. 6 —

THE REVISED CHARTER, 1830*

Louis Philippe, King of the French, to all present and to come, greeting.

We have ordered and do order that the Constitutional Charter of 1814, such as it has been amended by the two Chambers on August 7th and accepted by us on the 9th, shall be again published in the following terms:

PUBLIC LAW OF THE FRENCH

1. Frenchmen are equal before the law, whatever may be their titles and ranks.

2. They contribute, without distinction, in proportion to their fortunes, towards the expenses of the State.

3. They are all equally admissible to civil and military employments.

4. Their personal property is likewise guaranteed; no one can be prosecuted or arrested save in the cases provided by law and in the form which it prescribes.

5. Everyone may profess his religion with equal freedom and shall obtain for his worship the same protection.

6. The ministers of the Catholic, Apostolic, and Roman religion, professed by the majority of the French, and those of the other Christian sects, receive stipends from the State.

7. Frenchmen have the right to publish and to have printed their opinions, while conforming with the laws.

The censorship can never be re-established.

8. All property is inviolable, without any exception for that which is called national, the law making no distinction between them.

* Frank Maloy Anderson, *The Constitutions and Other Select Documents Illustrative of the History of France, 1789-1901.* Minneapolis, 1904, pp. 507-513.

9. The State can require the sacrifice of a property on account of a legally established public interest, but with a previous indemnity.

10. All investigations of opinions and votes given prior to the restoration are forbidden: the same oblivion is required from the tribunals and from citizens.

11. The conscription is abolished. The method of recruiting for the army and navy is determined by the law.

FORMS OF THE GOVERNMENT OF THE KING

12. The person of the King is inviolable and sacred. His ministers are responsible. To the King alone belongs the executive power.

13. The King is the supreme head of the State; he commands the land and sea forces, declares war, makes treaties of peace, alliance and commerce, appoints to all places of public administration, and makes the necessary rules and ordinances for the execution of the laws, without the power ever to suspend the laws themselves or to dispense with their execution.

Moreover, no foreign troops can be admitted into the service of the State except in virtue of a law.

14. The legislative power is exercised collectively by the King, the Chamber of Peers, and the Chamber of Deputies.

15. The proposal of laws belongs to the King, the Chamber of Peers, and the Chamber of Deputies.

Nevertheless every taxation law must be first voted by the Chamber of Deputies.

16. Every law shall be freely discussed and voted by the majority of each of the two Chambers.

17. If a project of law has been rejected by one of the three powers, it cannot be presented again in the same session.

18. The King alone sanctions and promulgates the laws.

19. The civil list is fixed for the entire duration of the reign by the first legislature assembled after the accession of the King.

OF THE CHAMBER OF PEERS

20. The Chamber of Peers is an essential part of the legislative power.

21. It is convoked by the King at the same time as the Chamber of Deputies. The session of the one begins and ends at the same time as that of the other.

22. Every meeting of the Chamber of Peers which may be held outside of the time of the session of the Chamber of Deputies is unlawful and of no validity, except the single case in which it is assembled as a court of justice, and then it can exercise only judicial functions.

23. The appointment of peers of France belongs to the King. Their number is unlimited: he can at his pleasure alter their dignities, appoint them for life, or make them hereditary.

24. Peers have entrance to the Chamber at 25 years of age, and a deliberative voice only at 30 years.

25. The Chamber of Peers is presided over by the Chancellor of France, and, in his absense, by a peer appointed by the King.

26. The princes of the blood are peers by right of their birth: they sit directly behind the president.

27. The sittings of the Chamber of Peers are public, as are those of the Chamber of Deputies.

28. The Chamber of Peers has jurisdiction over crimes of high treason and the attacks against the security of the State, which shall be defined by law.

29. No peer can be arrested except by the authority of the Chamber, nor be tried except by it in a criminal matter.

OF THE CHAMBER OF DEPUTIES

30. The Chamber of Deputies shall be composed of the deputies elected by electoral colleges whose organization shall be determined by law.

31. The deputies are elected for five years.

32. No deputy can be admitted to the Chamber unless he is 30 years of age and meets the other qualifications determined by the law.

33. If, however, there cannot be found in the department 50 persons of the required age who pay the amount of taxes determined by the law, their number shall be filled up from the largest taxpayers below this amount of tax, and these shall be elected together with the first.

34. No one is an elector, unless he is at least 25 years of age and meets the other conditions determined by the law.

35. The presidents of the electoral colleges are chosen by the electors.

36. At least one-half of the deputies shall be chosen from among the eligibles who have their political domicile in the department.

37. The president of the Chamber of Deputies is elected by it at the opening of each session.

38. The sittings of the Chamber are public; but the request of five members suffices for it to form itself into secret committee.

39. The Chamber divides itself into *bureaux* in order to discuss the propositions which have been presented to it by the King.

40. No tax can be imposed or collected, unless it has been consented to by the two Chambers and sanctioned by the King.

41. The land tax is consented to only for one year. Indirect taxes can be established for several years.

42. The King convokes the two Chambers each year: he prorogues them and can dissolve that of the deputies; but in that case he must convoke a new one within the space of three months.

43. No bodily constraint can be exercised against a member of the Chamber during the session nor in the preceding or following six weeks.

44. No member of the Chamber, during the course of the session, can be prosecuted or arrested upon a criminal charge, unless he should be taken in the act, except after the Chamber has permitted his prosecution.

45. No petition can be made or presented to either of the Chambers except in writing: the law forbids the bringing of them in person to the bar.

OF THE MINISTERS

46. The ministers can be members of the Chamber of Peers or the Chamber of Deputies.

They have, besides, their entrance into either Chamber and must be heard when they demand it.

47. The Chamber of Deputies has the right to accuse the ministers and to arraign them before the Chamber of Peers, which alone has that of trying them.

OF THE JUDICIARY

48. All justice emanates from the King: it is administered in his name by judges whom he appoints and whom he invests.

49. The judges appointed by the King are irremovable.

50. The courts and regular tribunals actually existing are continued; none of them can be changed except by virtue of a law.

51. The existing commercial court is retained.

52. The justice of the peace, likewise, is retained. Justices of the peace, although appointed by the King, are not irremovable.

53. No one can be deprived of the jurisdiction of his natural judges.

54. In consequence, extraordinary commissions and tribunals cannot be created, under any title or under any denomination whatsoever.

55. Criminal trials shall be public unless such publicity would be dangerous to order and morality; and, in that case, the tribunal shall declare it by a judicial order.

56. The system of juries is retained. Changes which a longer experience may cause to be thought necessary can be made only by a law.

57. The penalty of confiscation of property is abolished and cannot be re-established.

58. The King has the right of pardon and that of commuting penalties.

59. The Civil Code and the laws actually existing which are not in conflict with the present Charter remain in force until legally abrogated.

SPECIAL RIGHTS GUARANTEED BY THE STATE

60. Persons in active military service, retired officers and soldiers, pensioned widows, officers and soldiers, retain their ranks, honors and pensions.

61. The public debt is guaranteed. Every form of engagement made by the State with its creditors is inviolable.

62. The old nobility resume their titles, the new retain theirs. The King makes nobles at will; but he grants to them only ranks and honors, without any exemption from the burdens and duties of society.

63. The Legion of Honor is maintained. The King shall determine its internal regulations and its decoration.

64. The colonies are regulated by special laws.

65. The King and his successors shall swear, at their accession in the presence of the assembled Chambers, to observe faithfully the Constitutional Charter.

66. The present Charter and all the rights that it consecrates stand entrusted to the patriotism and the courage of the National Guards and of all French citizens.

67. France resumes its colors. For the future, no other cockade shall be worn than the tricolor cockade.

SPECIAL PROVISIONS

68. All the new appointments and creations of peers made during the reign of Charles X are declared null and void.

Article 23 of the Charter shall be submitted to a new examination in the session of 1831.

69. The following subjects shall be provided for successively by separate laws within the shortest possible space of time:

1st. The use of the jury for political and press offences;

2d. The responsibility of the ministers and the other agents of the [executive] power;

3d. The re-election of deputies appointed to public functions with salaries;

4th. The annual vote of the quota of the army;

5th. The organization of the National Guards, with the participation of the National Guards in the choice of their officers;

6th. Provisions which assure in a legal manner the status of the officers of every grade in the army and navy;

7th. Departmental and municipal institutions founded upon an elective system;

8th. Public instruction and the liberty of teaching;

9th. Abolition of the double vote and fixing of the electoral and eligibility conditions.

70. All laws and ordinances, wherein they are contrary to the provisions adopted for the reform of the Charter, are forthwith and shall remain annulled and abrogated.

We command all our courts and tribunals, administrative bodies, and all others that they keep and maintain, cause to be kept, observed and maintained the present Constitutional Charter, and to make it more known to all, that they cause it to be published in all the municipalities of the kingdom and wherever there shall be need; and in order that this may be firm and stable forever, we have caused our seal to be affixed thereto.

Done at the Palais Royal at Paris, the 14th day of the month of August, in the year 1830.

Signed,   Louis Philippe.

— Reading No. 7 —

A MUSICAL EVENING AT THE PALAIS ROYAL, MARCH, 1831 *

Count Rodolphe Apponyi (1802-1853) was a young Hungarian aristocrat. An attaché brought to the Paris embassy in 1826 by his cousin, the Austrian ambassador, he remained until 1850. Apponyi's daily journal was not published until long after his death.

✓   ✓   ✓

2 March, 1831.

* Journal du comte Rodolphe Apponyi, attaché de l'ambassade d'Autriche-Hongrie à Paris. Publié par Ernest Daudet. Vol. I, Paris, Plon-Nourrit, 1913, pp. 432-435, abridged. Reprinted by permission of the publishers.

As early as yesterday, one saw some of those sinister figures who, like birds before a storm, foreshadowed news for us. This morning a great number of rowdies went about the city or gathered on the squares. However, the authorities managed to disperse them.

This evening, we were invited to attend a grand concert at the Palais Royal; the idea was to throw dust in our eyes, as if there were not the slightest anxiety. However, the agitation in Paris increased from hour to hour. Although we were little inclined to listen to music while there was brawling in the streets, it was nevertheless necessary to do one's part and see that the invitations were not cancelled. So there we were embarked in our landau. . . .

. . . On the square of the Palais Royal the disorder was at its height; the crowd was being driven back with bayonets, and it, in turn victorious or vanquished, roared and jeered at the carriages. The square was lighted by torches, for the street lamps had been destroyed at the beginning of the riot, a fact which added more to the horror of the spectacle. All the way to the porch of the palace, hideous figures came up to the glass windows of our carriages, threatening the aristocrats. . . .

The king and queen received us as usual. However, from time to time, the king's aides-de-camp approached him, and the people who were around him tried to catch some of the information which was given in low voices, or else conjectures were formed on the basis of the king's facial expression while he was speaking with his aides-de-camp.

The vocalists entered pale and trembling and sang out of tune during a good half of the evening. Suddenly, the rumor went around that neither the line troops nor the National Guard could any longer resist the overwhelming odds. In fact, even through the sounds of the orchestra, one heard the shouts and frightful cries of an unruly populace which wanted, it was said, to come and plant the tree of liberty on the king's terrace. Even Her Majesty who, up to that time, had showed resolution, became anxious. She went near the casement windows to see what was happening in the courtyard and did not appear pleased with what she saw. . . .

However, the doors were opened and the king reappeared beaming.

—It is ended, he said, all is ended; the Chartres Hussars have dispersed the rioters.

It was told in confidence, discreetly, that the combat had been murderous, that more than 20 insurgents had been left on the square.

At our departure, the square and the streets were perfectly quiet; the troops were bivouacking around their fires and numerous patrols were moving through the city in every direction. . . .

— Reading No. 8 —

CASIMIR PERIER: POLICIES OF THE JULY MONARCHY, 1831 *

Casimir Perier (1777-1832), a rich banker, was a deputy under the Restoration and became Louis Philippe's prime minister in 1831-1832. See pp. 40-46. His descendants, one of them a president of the Third Republic, adopted Casimir-Périer as a surname.

✓   ✓   ✓

Chambre des Députés
Vendredi 18 *mars* 1831

M. Casimir Perier,
. . . When the king did me the honor of calling upon me to form and preside over his council, I thought that this council should be constituted on the basis of principles stated and agreed upon by all its members. . . . The day when this harmony ceases will be the day of its dissolution. . . .
. . . The principle of the July Revolution and consequently of the government which is derived from it is not insurrection. The principle of the July Revolution is resistance to governmental aggression. France was provoked; France was defied; it defended itself, and the victory is that of the law, unworthily outraged. Respect for oaths sworn to, respect for law, that, then, is the principle of the July Revolution; that is the principle of the government which it founded.
For it founded a government and did not inaugurate anarchy. It did not overturn the social order; it affected only the po-

* *Archives parlementaires de 1787 à 1860. Recueil complet des débats législatifs et politiques des chambres françaises* . . . sous la direction de M. J. Mavidal et de M. E. Laurent. . . . Second Series, Vol. LXVII, Paris, 1888, pp. 682-683, abridged.

litical order. It had for aim the establishment of a government free but orderly (Very good! Very good!). . . .

Internally our duty is simple. We have no great constitutional experiment to undertake. Our institutions were set in order by the Charter of 1830. . . .

The fact is . . . the trouble is in people's minds. Uneasy and divided, they accept all sorts of fears and suspicions. . . .

The cleverness of factions increases and exploits this kind of artificial terror. . . .

Our ambition is to re-establish confidence. . . .

Armed to defend its rights, France knows how to respect the rights of others. . . .

We desire that peace which is so necessary to liberty. We would want war, and we would wage it, if the security or honor of France were at stake; for then liberty would be menaced. . . .

Gentlemen, the principle of nonintervention has been posed: we adopt it; that is, we maintain that foreigners have no right of armed intervention in internal affairs. . . .

We will everywhere uphold the principle of nonintervention by means of negotiations. But only to safeguard the interest or the dignity of France would we take up arms. We concede to no people the right to force us to fight for its cause, and the blood of the French belongs only to France. . . . (Very good! Very good!)

— Reading No. 9 —

LOUIS PHILIPPE'S DAY, AS RECALLED BY COUNT MONTALIVET*

Marthe Camille Bachasson, comte de Montalivet (1801-1880), was a member of the Chamber of Peers who inherited his title in the 1820's. He served in a number of ministries under the July Monarchy and was an officer of the National Guard. Among his other duties, he administered the crown domains

* Comte de Montalivet, *Fragments et souvenirs*, Vol. 2, *1836-1848*. Paris, 1900, pp. 1-37, abridged.

*and supervised government expenditures on projects such as the
reconstruction of Versailles. Many of his recollections were
written long after the events, but there is no doubt concerning
his intimacy with the royal family.*

✔   ✔   ✔

From his accession to the throne on August 9, 1830, to
October 1, 1831, King Louis Philippe lived in the Palais Royal
that he had ardently wished never to leave. Politics as well as
prudence soon made very difficult, I ought to say impossible,
the prolongation of this stay. On the one hand, the aversion
of the King to residence in the Tuileries palace seemed to the
Parisians to be a sentiment not wholly consistent with the full
results of their victory in the July days. . . .

On the other hand, the Palais Royal was open and easily
approachable on all sides. . . . Royalty could be easily menaced there, and confined. . . .

The king arose a little after the queen, between seven-thirty
and eight o'clock in the morning. As soon as he was out of
bed, he spent several minutes in the queen's study to converse
with her about family affairs or about certain observations relative to the running of the palace.

That done, the king went to prepare himself for the day in
an adjacent room, where he would find his *valet de chambre,*
usually for form only, for he did not like to be served.

As soon as he was dressed, the king read the newly arrived
diplomatic dispatches, all of which were put into his hands
by the Minister of Foreign Affairs. . . . When there were no
dispatches, he read some English newspaper, usually the
Times; that was evidently for him another way of studying
Europe. But he made no point of reading French papers
to inform himself about internal politics, and—something to
be astonished at—I never saw him with a single one in his
hands. . . .

. . . In the mornings reserved for the civil lists, the only
affairs in which he was really interested were those which concerned the restoration of the palaces, the fine arts, and history
written with an artist's brush or sculptor's chisel. . . .

The king's afternoons were in the first place devoted to politics; it was the hour when some of the ministers came to work
alone with him. . . .

After the departure of the ministers, the king received company from time to time in the room. . . .

Up to the time of his accession, the king had been used to
much movement. Seated on the throne, he did not want to
change his habits; thus during the year he spent in the Palais
Royal, he tried to go out to make some purchases under the

palace arcades or even on the boulevards. He was obliged to give this up. Importunate ovations, inconsiderate curiosity, embarrassing demonstrations forced him to abstain. . . .

Physical activity was so necessary for his health that he had to search for ways to escape the confinement that politics imposed on him in the palaces of Paris. The terrace at the edge of the water was the one most often deserted; he had an underground passage made which permitted him to go there, escaping the stares of the public and the surveillance of the police; in winter it was there that he took some exercise.

The king often devoted the last portion of the afternoon to these promenades which maintained his health. . . .

In Paris, the king dined at six o'clock, and always at home. He had, from time to time, a small number of guests; but, each day, he received at his table the officers and chiefs of the National Guard. He went next into the family drawing room, beside which opened, to the north, a billiard room, and to the south, three rooms where the king had the habit of walking up and down, usually while conversing with some guest or visitor. He especially liked to receive ambassadors and heads of foreign legations, with whom he took pleasure in prolonging the conversation.

In the family drawing room, nothing attracted attention more than the queen's worktable, or rather the table over which she presided; around it were seated all the princesses, her daughters, and Madame Adelaide, who were soon joined by several of the princes. The queen and Madame did handiwork destined for the poor, interrupting it occasionally to welcome the small number of visitors who came each evening, and to listen joyfully to the conversation of the princes and princesses reflecting both the gaiety of youth and the wit of the best educated intellects. Now and then, between visitors, the king approached the queen's table and joined in the conversation with the same liveliness as his children. . . .

Neuilly and Saint-Cloud were the summer residences where the royal family stayed for the longest time. . . .

But let us get back to the Tuileries, where we have left the king departing about ten o'clock from the family parlor in order to go to his large study, while the queen, a few minutes later, retired into hers.

Madame Adelaide's hour had finally arrived; she would hurry to meet her brother, some woman's work in her hand, and would take a chair beside him: silent when an absorbing piece of work imposed silence on her brother, she was completely happy when the king interrupted himself to think out loud before her and with her. . . .

. . . Then, after these evenings devoted to friendship with

his sister and to his personal affairs, the king retired to the queen's bedchamber which was also his; at that moment he was finally going to take a well earned rest, on a kind of camp bed, which touched the queen's and whose hardness recalled the simplicity and austere habits which allowed him to preserve for so long his health of body and mind. . . .

— Reading No. 10 —

RÉMUSAT AND TOCQUEVILLE: PORTRAITS OF LOUIS PHILIPPE*

Charles François Marie, comte de Rémusat (1797-1875), and Alexis Henri Charles Clérel, comte de Tocqueville (1805-1859), were fellow academicians and deputies, whose memoirs were written with an obvious relish for nuances and details. Less famous than Tocqueville, Rémusat was at first a member of the conservative majority, but in the 1840's he became a member of the opposition which demanded parliamentary reform. Tocqueville's Souvenirs *were first published in 1893. Rémusat's* Mémoires *are the most interesting recent publication concerning the July Monarchy.*

✔   ✔   ✔

I. RÉMUSAT

Louis Philippe was a man of average height, sufficiently strong, agile and active, moving easily, his head high, but a little awkward because he was long-waisted. He had a large face with regular features, rather handsome on the whole, just

* Charles de Rémusat, *Mémoires de ma vie.* Vol. III, introduced and annotated by Charles H. Pouthas, Paris, Librairie Plon, 1960, pp. 493-498, abridged. Reprinted by permission of the publishers. *The Recollections of Alexis de Tocqueville.* Translated by Alexander Teixeira de Mattos and edited with additions by J. P. Mayer, New York, Columbia University Press, 1949, pp. 4-5. Reprinted by permission of the publishers.

right, one would have said, for the great wig of Louis XIV, to whom he bore a striking resemblance. . . .

The king's countenance in repose was rather impressive. His eyes, more animated than handsome, had an expression of shrewdness, good will, and gaiety. His aquiline nose . . . was the noblest and most royal of his features. His mouth, expressive and pleasant, was capable of mimicry which would have succeeded in the comedy theater. His facial expressions reflected his conversation. Vivacity, liveliness, and a certain good-natured roguishness, a joyous and informal animation, and in serious moments, the calm of tested courage rather than the flame of heroism—that is what his features expressed, reinforced by a varied and penetrating accent and by an involuntary and fluent imitation of those about whom he was speaking. His words, gestures, and bearing in public had little of majesty, and in moments of stress he did not gain in nobility. One recognized, in his conversation, if not a king, at least an important personage, a man whom birth and habits had formed for great situations, although his gravity was perpetually enlivened by outbursts and laughter with which he interrupted his most solemn speeches. The king lacked the very highest qualities of mind. He was not made for profound or sublime matters. The domain of the imagination was closed to him. But he possessed a splendid set of the more ordinary faculties. His prompt and lively intelligence was served by a great aptitude for work, provided he had some variety in his occupations. This intelligence was always alert, always pushing ahead, and rested only by passing from one thing to another. . . . He gave himself entirely to whatever he was doing. . . .

His outstanding faculty was perhaps his memory. From a long life, full of events, experiences, and travels, he had forgotten nothing. He learned easily and retained everything, but with neither classification nor method. . . . He spoke English, Italian, and Spanish fluently, and knew some German. . . .

. . . The rest of his knowledge—varied, often technical, always readily at hand—gave him a practical sense which was useful in conducting business. But he knew nothing systematically or in the modern manner. For, on the whole, the new ideas had kept, in his mind, their aspects of the end of the last century. He was a philosopher of Voltaire's time, brought up by Mme. de Genlis and nourished by his family on memories of the Old Regime. Hostile to the emigration, he shared some of its ideas, at least in judging France since 18 Brumaire. A pupil of Dumouriez and an admirer of England, he did not know the Empire and had no appreciation of the Emperor, whose qualities and defects were almost equally antipathetic to him. He judged him as a Tory of 1810 would have judged him.

And the pretensions and vanities of the new France inspired in him a kind of pity, although he knew how to cater to them when he had to, not without a trace of impatience and disdain. Basically he did not have much appreciation of peoples, except of the English, who alone seemed to him to be level-headed and capable. Although in his personal sentiments he was in full communion with French society, he had very British prejudices about its political and economic institutions and was forever deploring equality of inheritances and the impoverishment of the nation. He had not even brought from London a perfect understanding of the English constitution; he interpreted it in an exclusively monarchical sense and strongly doubted that it was suited to France, which he found too republican for it. He was faithful to his oath to uphold the constitution, more from discretion, duty, and necessity than from taste and conviction. . . .

. . . What he pardoned the least in the constitutional regime and its orthodox proselytes was the desire to efface him. He demanded on every occasion his share of influence and credit. . . . This was more vanity than ambition, for he had a high idea of himself, believed himself competent in everything, and could not bear anyone's pretension to do better, or anyone's failure to appreciate his superiority. . . .

. . . His tolerance and his clemency were without limits. I do not speak of the clemency which he showed to the enemies of his throne and his life, which some have judged excessive. Today it does honor to his memory and to his government. It calls attention to a spirit and mind which rose above anger and fear; and it was this generosity which made him much superior to the last Bourbons and to all the Bonapartes. . . .

II. TOCQUEVILLE

Although he came from one of the noblest families in Europe, he concealed all hereditary pride deeply in his soul; nevertheless, he certainly believed that there was no other human being like him. However, he had most of the qualities and defects which belong more particularly to the subaltern orders of society. He had regular habits and wanted those around him to have them too. He was orderly in his conduct, simple in his habits; his tastes were tempered; he was a born friend of the law, an enemy of all excesses, sober in his ways except in his desires. He was human without being sentimental, greedy or soft. He had no flaming passions, no ruinous weaknesses, no striking vices, and only one kingly virtue: courage. He was extremely polite, but not from choice or greatness—a politeness of a merchant rather than of a Prince. He hardly appreciated literature or art, but he passionately loved industry. His memory was prodigious and capable of retaining the minutest detail. His conversation was prolix, diffuse, original and trivial, anecdotal, full of small facts, of salt and meaning; it gave all satisfaction which one may find in intellectual pleasures when delicacy and elevation are absent. His mind was distinguished, but withdrawn and embarrassed, for his soul was neither high nor profound. He was enlightened, subtle, flexible; as he was only open to that which was useful, he was full of profound disdain for the truth, and he did so little believe in virtue that his sight was darkened. Thus he did not see the beauty which truth and decency show; he did not even understand any more their usefulness which they so often have. He had a profound knowledge of human beings, but he knew them only through their vices. He was an 18th century unbeliever in religious matters and a 19th century skeptic in politics; having no belief himself, he did not believe in the belief of others. . . .

— Reading No. 11 —

ARMAND MARRAST: "REPUBLICAN DOCTRINES, PROGRAM OF THE TRIBUNE," 1833*

Armand Marrast (1801-1852) was editor of the republican daily La Tribune, *which was heavily fined by the government and came to an end in 1835. Marrast was arrested after the insurrection of April, 1834, but escaped to England. He returned in 1836 to edit* Le National, *Carrel's old paper. He was prominent in the 1848 revolution.*

✓   ✓   ✓

The aim of the *Tribune* is social reform by means of the political instruments which influence a nation.

Social reform must work toward the most equitable distribution of the costs and benefits of society.

* Extrait de la "Tribune" du 31 janvier 1833. Paris, 1833, pp. 5-15, abridged.

Therefore it must destroy all institutions which establish shocking inequalities, and must create those which can raise to a condition as close as *possible* to perfect social equality those classes which today are the most mistreated. . . .

To arrive at this destination from our present point of departure there are two ways: one violent, that is, revolution; the other, peaceful education of public opinion. . . . The *Tribune* accepts both of them.

However, this is only temporary.

Until the present day it has been recognized that peoples, ceaselessly adding to their enlightenment and their industry, increase proportionally their material and moral needs. These needs spread, penetrate the masses, and when immovable institutions compress them and repulse them there comes a day when progress, in a kind of flood, defeats the opposing interests and takes its place in the sun at the cost of terrible dislocations.

This is what is meant by revolutions.

Revolutions are thus the explosion and victory of progress.

The honor of the present era is to have understood that instead of waiting until a revolution has given victory to progress it is necessary, on the contrary, that each day some progress be realized under a government accessible to all newly born and growing interests.

To this end, forms of government must be malleable, responsive to the movement of ideas, variable like the people's needs, and resistant only to the caprices of minorities.

Now the way to achieve and organize this constant progress of the people is for everything to be done by them and for them.

The most democratic form of government is clearly the republican.

The *Tribune* thus considers the *republic* to be the instrument which is best for progress and most adaptable to it, the instrument which makes future revolutions an impossibility. . . .

Sovereignty of the people is the submission of the interests and will of each citizen to the interests and will of all.

From this follows inescapably the submission of each part to all, of local powers to the central power, of all the separate wills to the single will of the nation. . . .

The national will and interests are formulated by the people assembled or by a body representative of the *whole* people.

The legislative power resides in this representation.

It must be unique, for the nation is one, and a *national will* cut in two is incomprehensible. Therefore there should not even be two legislative assemblies. . . .

However, to avoid either errors or undue influences on a single assembly, law projects will be prepared, discussed, and elaborated by a committee of inquiry. . . .

In this way would be satisfied the views of those several good minds who demand two degrees of discussion.

The executive power is subordinate, temporary, revocable, renewable by election, from the lowest to the highest degree of the hierarchy. . . .

The judicial power is part of the executive power. Irremovability of those who exercise it is incompatible with the sovereignty of the people, the more so since the jury, a constant emanation of society, already applied by our laws, must be extended to all litigation. . . .

Liberty of conscience, of opinion, freedom to manifest both of these unrestrictedly by means of press, associations, theaters, and all organs of thought, whatever they may be, are inalienable rights. . . .

Society owes to each of its members a complete moral education and sufficient instruction to aid in the development of his natural faculties.

Education must be universal, free of charge, and obligatory in so far as it is concerned with public morality. . . .

Moral principles have no frontiers. . . .

Peoples are brothers, as are individual men. . . .

The law of nations has no other end than the universal association of nations: an association already foreseen and called for by the superior intelligences who on our continent are working together for a *European republic.*

All diplomacy which does not look to this end is immoral.

War is an evil. . . .

. . . Economic society exists only through labor. . . .

Two great abuses today paralyze the effectiveness of labor: the assessment of taxes; the condition of credit.

Taxation is unjust; credit is not organized. . . .

For taxation to be equitably apportioned there should be a single tax. For it to be just, it must be in constant relation with wealth.

The tax must be progressive.

As for the organization of credit, it consists in arranging that any man in any location, if he offers the double guarantee of morality and labor, will have access to capital. . . .

It is association which must be organized, in order to bring about the gradual passing of the instruments of labor into the hands of those who labor.

To that end it is important, first, that the circulation of capital be increased by the organization of banks . . . and of all those credit establishments which should bring together the men who own the instruments of labor and those who work with them. . . .

Work engenders property, a right sacred like all the others, for it is born like the others of our faculties and our needs.

However, the right of property of each ceases at the point where this right harms the right of others. . . .

Thus the law can always interfere with property in the name of society as a whole. . . .

Thus the liberty of each individual which, left to itself, would engender license, halts before justice, which corrects it by means of equality. . . .

Armand Marrast

— Reading No. 12 —

LAW ON ASSOCIATIONS, APRIL 10, 1834*

This law, aimed at the small cells of the Droits de l'Homme *society and other such organizations, was part of the background of the insurrections of Lyon and Paris in April, 1834.*

✓ ✓ ✓

Art. 1. The provisions of article 291 of the Penal Code are applicable to associations of more than 20 persons, even when these associations are divided into sections of smaller numbers, and even if they do not assemble every day or on specified days.

A permit given by the government is always revocable.

2. Whoever is part of an unauthorized organization will be punished by imprisonment for two months to a year and a fine of 50 to 1000 francs.

In the case of a second offense, the penalties may be doubled. . . .

3. Those will be considered as accomplices and punished as such who have knowingly lent or rented their houses or apartments for one or several meetings of an unauthorized association. . . .

* J. B. Duvergier, *Collection complète des lois.* . . . Vol. 34, Paris, 1835, pp. 58-64, abridged.

— Reading No. 13 —

ALBAN DE VILLENEUVE-BARGEMONT: "ECONOMIE POLITIQUE CHRÉTIENNE," 1834*

Alban de Villeneuve-Bargemont (1784-1850) had a long career as a prefect, starting under Napoleon I. Under the July Monarchy he was a deputy and a member of the Academy of Moral and Political Sciences.

ˀ   ˀ   ˀ

Struck by the poverty which is devouring several European countries, and by its progress, which seems to advance parallel with that of modern civilization, we have wished to study its causes, determine its effects, and seek the remedies that are most suitable for ameliorating, in a lasting manner, the fate of the suffering and unhappy classes of society.

Everything is explained for us by the enchainment and strength of the principles which subject the social and material order to the eternal laws of the moral and religious order. Work and charity have seemed to us to be the two great bases of human societies, the only elements of general happiness, elements joined by Providence, which cannot be separated without destroying the harmony and the economy of the social universe.

It is in vain that the science which teaches how to create wealth analyzes and demonstrates clearly the power of work and industry. In neglecting the moral virtues in order to concentrate on material values, the English political economy has, to be sure, revealed to a few men the art of getting rich, but it has not been capable of resolving the problem of an equitable distribution of wealth. In placing the destiny of man in the narrow and gross sphere of the senses and of physical pleasure, it could indeed call forth cupidity, wants, and labor, but it destroyed all the links that should unite the rich and the poor; it dried up the sources of well-being of the working classes, i.e., sobriety, economy, prudence, and the adequacy of wages.

What the English political economy has, in our time, summed

* Vol. III, Paris, 1834, pp. 381-384, slightly abridged.

up in didactic precepts, modern philosophy had long since enshrined in doctrines. Both, being outgrowths of systematized egotism, developed, in different forms, the theory of material civilization, which ends by giving to a small minority the monopoly of industry and wealth, and by abandoning the masses to ignorance and to moral and physical privations. . . .

Such are the true causes of pauperism. For the fact must be faced that the ignorance and vices with which we reproach the poor are the necessary consequences of egoism and the example set by the rich. . . .

Egoism, centralizing industry for its own exclusive profit, brings inevitably in its wake the ignorance, immorality, sicknesses, improvidence, poverty, and finally revolt of the workers. Charity, on the contrary, provides as companions to industry, health, enlightenment, virtues, sobriety, moderation, sufficiency, and submission to the civil and moral laws.

These truths, concerning which we have tried to assemble multiple and unanswerable proofs, have led us to see in a religious system of popular education, in the spirit of association applied to charity, in the development of agriculture and industry which derives from it, and finally in the reform of the legislation which regulates industry and the administration of charity, the principal means of regenerating the fate of the poor and indigent classes.

— Reading No. 14 —

LAMENNAIS: A FABLE FROM "PAROLES D'UN CROYANT," 1834*

Chapter X of the Paroles d'un croyant *is a story, written in the first person, in which the author tells how he was feeling sad and oppressed by the evils of the world. Then God put him to sleep and sent a spirit to show him the meaning of history beyond time as we know it.*

* Félicité de Lamennais, *Paroles d'un croyant*. Second edition, Paris, 1834, pp. 49-56, abridged.

And the whole human race looked to me like a single man.

And this man had done much evil and little good, and had felt much sorrow and little joy.

And he was lying there in his misery on an earth now frozen, now burning, thin, famished, and ill, burdened by a weariness interspersed with convulsions, weighted down by chains forged in the dwelling place of demons. . . .

And this was man; I recognized him.

And there, a ray of light came from the east, and a ray of love from the south, and a ray of strength from the north.

And these three rays came together in the heart of this man. . . .

And then, what until that moment had seemed to be only one man appeared to me as a multitude of peoples and nations.

And my first impression had not been mistaken, and neither had my second.

And these peoples and nations, awakening on their bed of anguish, began to say to themselves:

Where do our sufferings and apathy come from, and the hunger and thirst which torment us, and the chains which bend us toward the earth and enter into our flesh?

And their intelligence opened and they understood that the sons of God, the brothers of Christ, had not been condemned by their father to slavery, and that this slavery was the source of all their ills.

Each then tried to break his irons, but no one succeeded.

And they looked at each other with a great pity and, love having acted within them, they said to each other: All of us have the same thought; must we not all have the same heart? Are we not all sons of the same God and brothers of the same Christ? Let us save ourselves or perish together.

And having said that, they felt within themselves a divine strength, and I heard their chains split, and they fought for six days against those who had enchained them, and on the sixth day they were victorious, and the seventh was a day of rest.

And the earth, which had been dry, turned green again, and all were able to eat of its fruits, and come and go without anyone saying to them: Where are you going? No one can pass this way.

And the little children picked flowers and brought them to their mothers, who gently smiled upon them.

And there were neither poor nor rich, but all possessed in abundance the things they needed, because all loved each other and aided each other as brothers.

And a voice like the voice of an angel resounded in the heavens: Glory to God, who has given intelligence, love, and strength to his children. Glory to Christ, who has given liberty to his brothers!

— Reading No. 15 —

ARMAND CARREL: THE CONTINUING DEMOCRATIC REVOLUTION, 1835 *

Armand Carrel (1800-1836) founded the newspaper Le National *with Adolphe Thiers and Auguste Mignet in 1830. After their departure Carrel and* Le National *became republican in January, 1832. Through no fault of Carrel, the following editorial appeared on the day of Fieschi's attack on Louis Philippe, described in Reading No. 16.*

⚜   ⚜   ⚜

Le National, July 28, 1835

. . . A revolution has been going on in France since '89 that tends to destroy all the governments of caste, of order, of robe, or of party, and to base the general well-being on the universal participation of the citizens in the administration of their affairs. . . .

This revolution . . . was satisfied neither by the experiment of constitutional monarchy in 1791, nor by the graduated democratic establishment of 1795, and for a moment it appeared to perish from the coup of 18 Brumaire. From that day to the events of 1814, it had given little sign of life, it must be admitted, and yet it had been alive in people's interests and in their hearts; it had secretly undermined the throne which collapsed before foreign invasion without being defended; and if the two invasions of 1815 have not dishonored and crushed France forever, it is because she had succeeded in separating her cause from that which had robbed her of her liberty. . . .

That which was paid for in 1830 by the glorious blood of Parisians is obtained and will not be called into question. In

* Armand Carrel, *Oeuvres politiques et littéraires.* Vol. 4, Paris, 1858, pp. 305-311, abridged.

July were ousted the remains of the old aristocracy, the ecclesiastical power, and the military feudality which were trying to undo the concessions of 1814 or to exploit for their benefit the rough outline of a representative government born of those concessions. The revolutionary forces of that time were composed of a majority of those bourgeois who had been admitted to the representative system of the senior branch, of what remained of the old servants of the Empire neglected by the Restoration, and finally of that popular mass which belonged to the imperial regime only by conscription and to the Restoration only as taxable and exploitable material.

The revolution would have been ended if it had been possible to extract from the July battle a government which gave a share of action to all these elements. Either because this was not possible or was not wanted, it happened, quite the contrary, that the popular mass . . . was still denied political participation, first by fine words, promises, and exhortations for patience, and then by cannon and cavalry charges. . . . It happened that the bourgeoisie, merely represented under the Restoration, yielded to the vain pride of becoming a government in its turn and of copying with pitiable servility and poverty of invention the pretentions, the mannerisms, the principles, the language, and the vices of the aristocratic classes which it had played a part in conquering.

Thus there was need for the democratic immensity, depository of the revolutionary idea in its broadest and most equitable sense, to dispossess the bourgeois monopoly as had been done with the aristocratic monopoly. This second judgment has been pronounced and will be executed more easily than the first, when the bourgeois monopoly has had recourse, in order to perpetuate itself, to the same attempts which marked the last day of the Restoration. . . .

There is, then, cause for everyone to rejoice on the anniversary of the 28th of July. Let those rejoice who would never have come to govern their country without the overthrow of the elder branch; it is very natural. But that others, in much larger numbers, find in the magnificent memories of the great day of the great week the certitude that the future belongs to them: that also is very natural. . . .

JOINVILLE: FIESCHI'S INFERNAL MACHINE, 1835*

(*Concerning Joinville, see Reading No. 1.*)

❦   ❦   ❦

The acts of aggression directed against my father without intermission were no laughing matter. . . . The most serious was that of Fieschi, on July 28, 1835. I, with my two older brothers, was to accompany the King to a review of the National Guard and army, drawn up on the boulevards. We had all been brought together beforehand, . . . when M. Thiers, Minister of the Interior, rushed in like a tornado and, signaling to my two brothers and me, led us into the alcove of the casement window.

"My dear Princes," he said, looking at us over the tops of his glasses, "it is more than likely that there will be an assassination attempt against your father, the King, today. This has come to us from several sources. There is talk of an explosive engine in the neighborhood of the Ambigu theatre. . . . We have had all the houses in the neighborhood of the Ambigu searched this morning. Nothing! Should the King be warned? Should the review be called off?" We unanimously answered that the King should be warned, but that he, well-known for his courage, would never consent to countermanding the review. . . .

The review went rather well, except that we all observed the presence of numerous individuals with insolent airs, all wearing red flowers in their buttonholes; evidently the members of secret societies, forewarned, not of what was going to happen, but to be ready for any eventuality. We had been able to take no precautions other than to keep a close watch, my brothers and I and the service aides, around the King. One of us and an aide took turns keeping immediately behind his horse, with our eyes on the troops and the crowd, in order to block out any suspicious movement. It was my turn to hold this position of surveillance . . . when, quite near the Ambigu, not the

* [François], Prince de Joinville, *Vieux souvenirs, 1818-1848*. Paris, 1894, pp. 84-88, abridged.

present theatre of that name whose neighborhood had been searched but an old abandoned Ambigu opposite the café of the Turkish Garden, a shot like that of a firing squad or canister was heard, and lifting my eyes at the sound I saw smoke in front of a window half closed by a blind.

I did not have time to see more, and I did not even notice right away that my neighbor on the left, Colonel Rieussec, had been killed, that Heymès, riddled with shot in his apparel, had his nose blown off, nor that my horse was wounded. I only saw my father holding his left arm and heard him say to me over his shoulder: "I have been hit." He had been, in fact; a ball had grazed the skin on his forehead, a spent ball had made the bruise about which he was complaining, and another had struck the neck of his horse. But we knew that only after the event; also we did not know until afterward that the instrument of the crime was a machine. Our first thought was that the shooting would continue; I dug my spurs into the belly of my horse and, seizing my father's horse by the bridle, while my two brothers hit it on its hind sides with their swords, we hurried him away from the immeasurable confusion which prevailed: horses without riders or horses carrying unsteady wounded, the ranks broken, men in working clothes rushing toward my father, to touch him or his horse, with frantic shouts of "Long live the King." As we withdrew, I saw the assault on the house from which the firing had come: the young aides-de-camp had jumped from their horses and together with the municipal guard and the police constables scaled the house and its neighbor, the café *Barfetti*. . . .

After that the review went on. We ascertained that neither the King nor ourselves had been wounded, but we were still unaware of the large number and names of the victims. . . . We made a calculation as we marched: 42 dead or wounded. . . . From the scene of the crime to the end of the line of troops was not far; the procession then turned around. The roadway was nothing but a pool of blood at the spot where the attack had taken place; the wounded and nearly all the dead had already been taken away and I saw only one corpse, face down in the mud, in the midst of the dead horses. . . . The review ended, and the imperturbability of my father was put to a harsh test by the unanimity and the violence of the acclamations in his behalf on the part of all—the crowd and the soldiers. It is unnecessary to add that we no longer saw any red *boutonnières*.

GUIZOT ON THE "JUSTE MILIEU," 1835 *

During the debates on the September Laws (see Reading No. 18), Guizot defended the following perspective.

✔   ✔   ✔

                    Chamber of Deputies, Session of August 28, 1835.

M. Guizot:

. . . We have undertaken for five years many things that were said to be impossible, many things which have ruined other governments. . . . And nevertheless, gentlemen, we have succeeded; and not only have we succeeded, but we have strengthened ourselves. . . .

Why, gentlemen? For two reasons.

The first is that France has obtained and possesses today, in the matter of guarantees and political liberties, everything that she has wanted since 1789, all that she will have need of for a long time to come: she no longer demands, just now, to conquer anything; she asks only to enjoy in peace what she possesses. We support France in this wish, which is her true wish; that is why she sustains us.

Moreover, gentlemen, France needs a government without mental reservations; and that is the position of the July government. All the governments which preceded it have had, in regard to the country's liberties, in regard to its institutions, mental reservations. . . . The Empire wanted absolute power; the Restoration wanted the old regime. The present government wants only things as they now are; all that it says, it thinks; all that it wishes, it wishes sincerely; nothing less, nothing more: it wants the Charter, nothing but the Charter. It is sincere, fully sincere in its relations with the country; it has its heart on its sleeve with France. . . .

But someone has said to us: "You will be obliged to go further; you will be pushed into a state of tyranny; you will not stop at suppressing the illegal, unconstitutional, anticonstitutional press; you will go on to interfere with the legitimate

* François Guizot, *Histoire parlementaire de France.* Vol. II, Paris, 1863, pp. 443-445, abridged.

press, with the opposition press of all parties—the opposition which is within constitutional limits."

No, Gentlemen; just as our thoughts and our intentions do not go that far, neither will our actions go beyond our thoughts. . . . Things like that are good to say to the parties who are obedient to absolute principles, . . . to our adversaries, to the absolutist and revolutionary factions . . . incapable of compromise and of moderation. But our own policy, gentlemen, the policy of the golden mean (*juste milieu*) is essentially hostile to absolute principles, to consequences pushed too far. . . . It is the nature of our policy to be an enemy of all excesses, to face about without the least embarrassment, without the least inconsistency, in order to combat now the one, now the other. . . . That is what makes our strength; that is why we are not afraid of being pushed to some excess which is repugnant and which has always been contrary to the system which we practice. (*From the center:* very good! very good!). . . .

— Reading No. 18 —

PRESS LAW, SEPTEMBER 9, 1835 *

The "September Laws" of 1835 which followed Fieschi's attack consisted of measures that facilitated prosecutions and condemnations (e.g., juries to decide by simple majority), and of the following concerning public expressions of opinion.

✓   ✓   ✓

. . . 2. The insulting of the King . . . when it has as its object to arouse hate or scorn of his person or of his constitutional authority, is an offense against the security of the state. . . .

4. Whoever places on the King the blame or responsibility for the acts of his government shall be punished with imprisonment of a month to a year and a fine of 500 to 5000 francs.

5. Any attack against the principle or form of the government established by the Charter of 1830, as they are defined by

---

* J. B. Duvergier, *Collection complète des lois.* . . . Vol. 35, Paris, 1835, pp. 255-271, abridged.

the law of November 29, 1830, is an attack on the security of the state, when it has as its object to incite to the destruction or to the changing of the government. . . .

7. Those persons shall be punished with the penalties provided by the preceding article who shall have adhered publicly to any other form of government, whether it be in attributing the rights to the French throne to persons banished in perpetuity by the law of April 10, 1832, or to any other than Louis Philippe I and his descendants;

whether it be in taking the title of republican or any other incompatible with the Charter of 1830;

whether it be in expressing the wish, the hope or the threat of the destruction of the constitutional monarchical order, or of the restoration of the fallen dynasty. . . .

11. It is forbidden to open or announce publicly subscriptions having as their object compensation for the fines, expenses, damages, and interest pronounced by judicial sentences. . . .

13. The bond that the owners of every journal or periodical are required to furnish shall be deposited, in cash, in the Treasury, which will pay the interest at the rate set for bonds. . . .

15. Each managing director responsible for a magazine or periodical must own, in his own private name, a third of the bond. . . .

20. No design, no engravings, lithographs, medals and stamps, no emblem of whatever nature and kind may be published, exposed, or put on sale without preliminary authorization of the Ministry of the Interior, at Paris, and of the prefects, in the departments. . . .

21. There may not be established, either in Paris or in the departments, any theatre or entertainment, of any nature whatever, without the preliminary authorization of the Minister of the Interior, at Paris, and of the prefects, in the departments.

The same authorization will be required for the plays which are presented there. . . .

— Reading No. 19 —

LAMARTINE: "FRANCE IS BORED!" 1839*

Alphonse de Lamartine (1790-1869) had been a deputy since 1834.

↗   ↗   ↗

Chamber of Deputies, Jan. 10, 1839.

M. de Lamartine:

. . . There is no majority here because there is not one in the country, because there is not one among the electors; there is no majority here because there is neither great action nor a great directing idea in the government since its origin in 1830. . . . 1830 has not succeeded in creating its action or finding its idea. You could not remake legitimacy; the ruins of the Restoration were under your feet. You could not create military glory; the Empire had passed, leaving you only a bronze column in a public square in Paris. The past was closed to you; you needed a new idea. . . . You have let the country lack action. You must not suppose, gentlemen, that because we are fatigued from the great movements which have shaken the century and ourselves everyone is as tired as we and fears the slightest movement. The new generations growing up behind us are not tired, not they; they want to act and grow tired in their turn: what action have you given them? France is a nation suffering from boredom!

And take care, the boredom of peoples easily leads to upheaval and ruin.

The following idea I am not going to develop; it is a whole system in itself. I shall content myself with identifying it. It is the idea of the masses, the idea of the organization and moralization of the people, taken in its largest sense. This government was born of the people; it should belong to them; it should be the constituent government of the interests of the greatest number. Yes, there you have in my opinion the mission of a new government of the 19th century. (Lively support from the left. Agitation.)

* *Archives parlementaires . . . Deuxième série (1800-1860).* Vol. CXXIII, Paris, 1911, p. 161.

Then you would have had stable majorities and minorities and an impulsion capable of making you resolve all these miserable parliamentary difficulties.

There lay safety, Gentlemen; an action and an idea: there lay strength. . . .

— Reading No. 20 —

LOUIS NAPOLEON BONAPARTE: "NAPOLEONIC IDEAS," 1839*

. . . The Emperor Napoleon contributed more than anyone else to the acceleration of the reign of liberty by saving the moral influence of the revolution and by diminishing the fears which it inspired. [*Footnote omitted*.] Without the Consulate and the Empire the revolution would have been nothing more than a great drama leaving behind fine memories but few other traces. . . . Napoleon planted in France and introduced everywhere in Europe the principal benefits of the great crisis of 1789, and because—to use his own expressions—*he cleansed the revolution, strengthened the kings*. . . . cleansed the revolution by separating its triumphant truths from the raging passions which had obscured them; he strengthened the kings by making government once more honored and respectable; he ennobled the peoples by making them aware of their power and giving them the kind of institutions that dignify man in his own eyes. The Emperor must be considered the Messiah of the new ideas; for, it must be said, in the immediate aftermath of a social overturn, the important thing is not to apply principles in all their theoretical subtlety but . . . to become one with the sentiments of the people, and to direct them boldly toward the aim which they wish to attain. To be capable of accomplishing such a task, *your very substance must respond to that of the people;* you must feel as they do, and your interests must be so fused with theirs that you and they can only vanquish or fall together! . . .

To sum up the imperial system one can say that its founda-

* *Des Idées napoléoniennes par le Prince Napoléon-Louis Bonaparte.* Paris, 1860, pp. 25-27, 105-108, 145-146, 150, 162.

tion is democratic, since all the powers come from the people, while its organization is hierarchical, since there are in society various grades to stimulate all degrees of ability.

The competition is open to 40 million people; merit alone distinguishes them from each other; the various degrees on the social scale reward them. . . .

To replace, among the European nations, the state of nature by a social state, such was, therefore, the thought of the Emperor; all of his political combinations tended toward this great result; but to achieve this end, it was necessary to bring England and Russia around to the sincere support of his views.

"So long as there is fighting in Europe," said Napoleon, "it will be a civil war." . . .

. . . The policy of the Emperor, on the contrary, consisted of founding a solid European association, in basing his system on whole nationalities and on the satisfaction of general interests. . . .

Especially loved by the common people, could Napoleon fear to give political rights to all citizens? When, upon being named Consul for Life, he re-established the principle of the right of election, he pronounced these remarkable words: "In the interest of the *stability* of the government, the people must have a greater part in elections." . . .

In concluding, let us repeat, the Napoleonic idea is not an idea of war, but a social idea—an industrial, commercial, humanitarian idea. If for some men it always appears surrounded by the thunder of combat, the reason is that it was indeed too long enveloped in the smoke of cannon and the dust of battles. But today the clouds have vanished, and one can see across the glory of arms a civil glory which is greater and more lasting.

— Reading No. 21 —

"L'ATELIER," NO. 1, SEPTEMBER, 1840*

L'Atelier *appeared between 1840 and 1850, usually about once a month. Its tendency was Christian socialist in the manner of Philippe Buchez (1796-1865), who knew the founders.*

* L'Atelier; organe des intérêts moraux et matériels des ouvriers. No. 1er, Septembre 1840, pp. 1-3, abridged.

The journal whose first number we deliver to the public today is addressed to workers by workers. In taking up the pen, we will not quit the workshop; we will remain what we have been up to this moment: sharing the sentiments and the labors of those to whom and for whom we are going to speak. . . .

Until today, the working classes have been championed by men who were unconnected with them. . . .

It will be necessary, therefore, for us to prove, when we speak of ourselves, that we are the vanguard of the workers, and that we are protesting, not for ourselves alone, but for labor, for industry, for all those who, like us, live each day from the bread earned the day before; it will be necessary to prove that the reorganization of labor is not merely an industrial question, but even a political problem, and then we shall have to demonstrate all the miseries which plague the greater part of the people, all the troubles which undermine their bodies and destroy their souls, all those adversities which leave them deprived of education, handed over to the evil counsels of hunger and the bad example set by the rich. . . .

Perhaps some of our readers will think that we speak very badly of subjects which are beyond our comprehension; but the point is, we know by experience the worth of moral things as well as that of political things. We feel the consequences of all the evil which is done as well as of all the evil which is spoken; we are subject to actual practice which cannot leave us in doubt. . . .

But if success crowns our good intentions, we shall have given the working classes the greatest possible service. We shall have proved that the workers are not only capable of practicing fraternity and loyalty, but that they are worthy also of liberty and equality, worthy of political rights, worthy of being emancipated from the industrial servitude under which they live. And if we demonstrate that emancipation is possible, if we show the means, who could refuse us the practice? . . .

Really there are only two parties in France, the radical party and the conservative party. . . .

Let us not believe, however, that these two parties embrace the whole nation, for if that were true, the question would soon be settled; the devourers of the budget are reckoned at barely a few thousand, while the exploited number millions. The struggle, obviously, would not be long and its outcome would not be in doubt.

Unfortunately, that is not the case. The majority, it must be confessed, is not of any party; for the moment it is indifferent and passive, as if nothing that happens concerns it. . . .

Moreover, it has a horror of everything resembling politics. . . . It has seen many revolutions take place without having gained much of anything, except a fresh outbreak of taxes; it has constantly shed its blood for the fatherland without reaping anything. . . .

The word *revolution* signifies for it trickery, deceit, lying, new exploitation with the help of grand words. . . .

Those, therefore, were completely in error who, despairing of overcoming legally the government's resistance to progress, attempted to overthrow it.

Those, therefore, are right who have abandoned the rifle of the insurgent to take up the pen of the petitioner. . . .

However, the radical party, the one which wants a revolution brought about peacefully, the reformist party, in short, has barely enough strength to sustain the struggle against the privileged, for those people decide everything: the budget, and consequently most of the press; the police, and . . . the political administration of the kingdom. . . .

But what makes the task of the radicals even more difficult is the indifference of the masses, an indifference which stems from failure, as yet, to understand the significance of the word *politics*. . . .

To overcome this repugnance in the working class, to make it understand little by little that its political rights are not empty words, that by them alone it can succeed in achieving the well-being that it wants, such is one of the thoughts of this publication. . . .

But first of all we reserve for ourselves the exposure in detail of the vices of our social organization, the explaining of how it comes about that the workers die of hunger beside immense fortunes; how it comes about that the masses degenerate in body and spirit as a result of excessive and poorly paid labor. . . .

As temporary palliatives, we will promote among the workers societies of mutual aid for sickness or unemployment; next we will transform them into provident societies; then eventually these associations will assure the worker a retirement pension, justly due to a worker as to a soldier, for both have equally served their country.

Little by little we will witness a decrease in the exploitation of man by man; gradually the possessors of capital will lose the privilege of living from the work of those who possess only their hands. We will obtain this result by promoting the establishment of *industrial associations* of workers, a principle already stated, but which has not yet been developed in a popular form. . . .

The means of making the people sovereign is to arrange for its participation in the making of the laws, which will be all the better for their being made by the people and for the people. . . .

The means therefore is electoral reform, demanded by the legal procedures of the petition.

Since it is probable that our demand will still suffer some delays, that in the meantime our miseries will still be the same, and since, moreover, we are far from believing that universal suffrage will cure them all at once, we must, then, consider how to create for ourselves a better present time; we will attain it by means of Association, at first on a small scale, then enlarged successively.

Confidence, devotion, and our cause is won!

— Reading No. 22 —

VICTOR HUGO: "1840, FUNERAL OF NAPOLEON, DECEMBER 15, NOTES MADE ON THE SPOT"*

I heard the call to arms in the streets starting at 6:30 in the morning. I set out at 11:00. The streets are deserted, the shops closed. . . . It is very cold; a bright sun, with light mists in the sky. The gutters are frozen.

. . . I emerge on the square of the Invalides. . . . I show my ticket for the first platform on the left. . . .

These platforms are immense scaffoldings which cover all the grass plots of the esplanade from the *quai* to the iron gate of the domed building. . . .

. . . On the two sides of the avenue two rows of heroic figures, colossal, pale in this cold sun, create a rather beautiful effect. They appear to be of white marble. But this marble is plaster. At the far end, opposite the dome, the statue of the emperor, in bronze. This bronze is also plaster. In each space between the statues, a pillar of color-printed and gilded fabric in rather bad taste is surmounted by a fire pot—full of snow for the moment. Behind the statues, the platforms and the crowd; between the statues, the national guardsmen scattered about; above the platforms, masts at the top of which 60 long tricolored pennants float magnificently. . . .

* Victor Hugo, *Choses vues*. Vol. III, Paris, 1887, pp. 17-31, abridged.

All eyes are fixed on the corner of the Quai d'Orsay from which the cortege must emerge. The cold increases the impatience. White and black smoke rises here and there through the misty mass of the Champs-Elysées, and distant explosions are heard.

All of a sudden the national guardsmen hurry to take up arms. An ordinance officer crosses the avenue at a gallop. Ranks form along the sides. Workmen put up ladders to the pillars and begin lighting the fire pots. A salvo of heavy artillery bursts forth loudly at the eastern corner of the Invalides. . . . The cortege approaches.

It is 12:30.

At the very end of the esplanade, toward the river, a double row of horse grenadiers with yellow straps, debouch solemnly. It is the constabulary of the Seine. That is the head of the cortege. At this moment the sun does its duty and appears magnificently. We are in the month of the battle of Austerlitz.

After the fur caps of the *gendarmerie* of the Seine appear the copper helmets of the municipal guard of Paris, then the lancers' tricolored pennants blowing in the wind in a charming manner. Fanfares and drums. . . .

The cortege, with generals and marshals intermingled, is a wonderful sight. The sun, striking the breastplates of the *carabiniers,* lights up a dazzling star on all their chests. The three military schools pass with proud and serious faces. Then the artillery and the infantry, as if they were going forth into battle; the caissons have spare wheels at their rear, the soldiers have packs on their backs. . . .

The mounted National Guard appears. Hubbub in the crowd. It is in rather good order, however; but it is a troop without glory, and that makes a gap in such a cortege. Someone laughs. . . .

Suddenly the cannons burst forth all at once aimed at three different points of the horizon. This threefold simultaneous noise encloses the ears in a sort of formidable and superb triangle. Faraway drums sound a salute.

The hearse of the emperor appears.

The sun, veiled up to this moment, reappears at the same time. The effect is prodigious.

One sees in the distance, in the mist and sun, on the gray and reddish-brown background of the trees on the Champs-Elysées, through the line of tall white statues, which resemble phantoms, moving slowly, a kind of golden mountain. . . . An immense clamor envelops this apparition. It could be said that this chariot draws after it the acclamation of the whole city as a torch trails its smoke. . . .

. . . The vehicle advances slowly. One begins to distinguish its shape. . . .

. . . Almost directly in front of it is the staff of the *Belle-Poule*, commanded by the Prince of Joinville on horseback. The Prince of Joinville's face is covered with a beard (blond), which seems to me to be contrary to naval regulations. . . .

Directly in front of me—I do not know what momentary obstacle has appeared—the hearse stops. It halts for several minutes between the statue of Jeanne d'Arc and that of Charles V.

I can examine it as I wish. The general effect has grandeur. It is an enormous mass, completely gilded, whose tiers go pyramiding above the four huge golden wheels which carry it. Under the violet crape bestrewn with bees, which covers it from top to bottom, are some rather fine details: the startled eagles of the substructure, the 14 victories of the summit, bearing on a golden table a semblance of a coffin. The true coffin is invisible. It has been placed in the vault of the substructure, which lessens the emotion. . . .

*   *   *

The spectators in the stands have not ceased stamping their feet until the moment the car catafalque is opposite them. Then only are the feet silent. One feels that a great emotion is passing through this crowd.

It is three o'clock. A salvo of artillery announces that the ceremony has just been completed within the Invalides. . . .

The words spoken were simple and grand. The Prince of Joinville said to the king: *Sire, I present to you the body of the emperor Napoleon.* The king responded: *I receive it in the name of France.* . . .

— Reading No. 23 —

ALEXANDRE AUGUSTE LEDRU-ROLLIN, CAMPAIGN SPEECH, 1841 *

Alexandre Auguste Ledru-Rollin (1808-1875) achieved prominence as a defense attorney for various republicans before being elected to the Chamber in 1841. He was also to be prominent in the 1848 Revolution.

* *Chambre des Députés. Elections.* 1839-1841, pp. 1-4, abridged.

Speech to the voters of Mans, July 24, 1841

Gentlemen,

. . . The sovereignty of the people, there you have the great principle which our fathers proclaimed nearly 50 years ago. But what has become of this sovereignty? Relegated to the formulas of a constitution, it has disappeared from the realm of facts. For our fathers, the people were the entire nation, each man enjoying an equal share of political rights, as God created for him an equal share of air and of sun. Today, the people are a herd guided by a few privileged beings like you, like me, gentlemen, who are called electors, and then by still other privileged people who are given the title of deputies.

And if this people, who are not represented, rise in order to claim their rights, they are thrown into prison.

If they form an association, in order not to perish from misery and to extend their insufficient wages, they are thrown into prison.

If, as at Lyons, in the days of mournful memory, they write on their standard: "bread or death," they are shot down, and their mutilated remains are slandered.

And to these cries of despair, some voices are heard responding from the platform: people, what do you want? What do you demand? Are you not sovereign, people, are you not king? Insulting derision, miserable irony! The people, king! They called him king also, the Pharisees of another epoch, this revealer of a new religion who came to preach to men about equality and brotherhood. They called him king, while whipping him, while crowning him with thorns, while throwing insult and blasphemy in his face. The people, gentlemen, is the *ecce homo* of modern times, but be convinced that their resurrection is near. They too will descend from the cross to demand an accounting of those who have too long ignored them. . . .

. . . It is enough to say that this dishonorable system, eaten by corruption, has outlived its time and must be changed, or we face violent revolution. In order to change it, gentlemen, electoral reform is the first step to take. . . . This reform must be radical, so that every citizen may be an elector; so that the deputy will belong to the nation, and not to wealth; so that he will be chosen for his virtue.

. . . The country requires more. . . . Political regeneration can therefore be only a step and a means of arriving at just social betterment. It is by this fraternal and sympathetic tendency, gentlemen, . . . that the Democratic party distinguishes itself especially and profoundly from the other parties germinated by the July Revolution.

Consider, in fact, the Doctrinaire phalange. . . . It invokes a kind of fictitious legitimacy which has neither the sanction of the people nor the sanction of old traditions. . . .

The Thiers party . . . sees in the July Revolution only a charter contracted in place of a charter granted . . .

Let us speak about the Barrot faction, which is no more than a gradation of the Thiers party . . . less corrupt than the latter . . . the friend of a certain dim liberalism. . . .

And the Legitimist party, which pretends to be advancing today in the name of the people . . . it affects our principles, and our language, and speaks of sovereignty of the people. . . . But . . . it is the fox who clothes himself, by necessity, in the lion's skin.

To these out-of-date or bastard parties, the people is a word only. . . .

For us, gentlemen, the people is everything. . . .

Which of us, indeed, while traveling through our manufacturing cities . . . has not felt himself deeply moved . . . by the sight of these men deprived of all pleasures, and scarcely finding in the wages of . . . work without rest the means to satisfy their most pressing needs? Of the young girls, earning six sous a day, and reduced to seeking through a cold and systematic prostitution the sustenance which they lack? Of those weak and languishing children, condemned prematurely to finding, in work beyond their strength, the bread which the father cannot get for them? . . .

Ah, well, gentlemen, in view of these shameful sores of our society . . . what does the representative government do?

In the Chamber, and to speak only of the last session, one busies oneself with the address. . . .

Then comes the Eastern Question: remembering the Pyramids, a short and glorious epoch, France feels young again . . . but one discourses, one negotiates, one temporizes, and the English, during this time, bombard Beyrouth, take Saint-Jean-d'Acre, and the tricolored flag is insulted, and France, bent double before the foreign power, expelled from the council of kings, sees its glory tarnished. . . .

. . . The fortifications obtained to stem foreign invasion are . . . directed against the liberties of France.

That is all there was for this session! . . .

And the press, has it not been hemmed in on all sides . . . in virtue of the laws of September . . . ?

. . . I know that these doctrines of dedication are treated as folly by the majority controlled by all the ministries. . . .

. . . But if the burning desire to dedicate oneself is sufficient for success, believe, gentlemen, that you will not have armed a soldier unworthy of this grand cause of democracy. . . .

COUNT APPONYI: THE DEATH OF THE DUKE OF ORLEANS, 1842 *

(Concerning Count Apponyi, see Reading No. 7.)

✓   ✓   ✓

July 26, 1842

The King has just opened the Chambers, to have voted the law relative to the regency, an urgent law, for Louis Philippe is a septuagenarian. What a shocking occurrence on the thirteenth of this month! What an unforeseen event, inconceivable, staggering! A handsome young prince, agile, admirably well-built, full of health, life, and future prospects, surrounded by tokens of esteem, of respect, of friendship, of love, adored son, idolized husband, cherished brother, father of two charming children, heir apparent of a powerful empire; this prince, I say, . . . is taking a drive in a carriage between the entrance of the Bois de Boulogne and the avenue of the Chateau de Neuilly; he falls from the carriage like a child of three, his head against the pavement; he stays in that spot, his skull fractured, without uttering a cry, without regaining consciousness, without being able to account for the immeasurable passage he has just made, . . . without . . . a word of love, a word of regret to his relatives, without being able to say a last good-by, without any transition from life to death! . . .

The coachman regains control of the horses, after several seconds of quick running, stops them, and seeing that the prince, whose agility is well known to him, is out of the carriage, returns to put himself again at the disposition of the Duke of Orleans. These few seconds were sufficient, alas! to plunge into mourning the royal family and all those who love him and are devoted to him!

What projects vanished, what calculations deceived!

Poor Duchess of Orleans! What has she not lost all at once: A handsome and gallant husband, the father of her children,

* *Journal du comte Rodolphe Apponyi, attaché de l'ambassade d'Autriche-Hongrie à Paris. Publié par Ernest Daudet.* Vol. III, Paris, Plon-Nourrit, 1913, pp. 475-479, abridged. Reprinted by permission of the publishers.

a friend full of devotion, a witty and pleasant companion, the supporter of her livelihood, and, with all that, a crown and her hopes! . . .

No one has any idea of the despair of the entire royal family. It would be vain for me to try to describe it. Nevertheless the King and Queen showed, at the very moment, a surprising moral strength. . . .

Happily, the King, in spite of his grief, had kept his strong and industrious head. He concerned himself, therefore, as soon as he had arrived at the Chateau de Neuilly, with affairs of state; he convened the Council of Ministers and decided at once the convocation of the Chambers in order to have them vote a law of regency in favor of the Duke of Nemours. . . .

— Reading No. 25 —

A LETTER FROM ALGERIA, 1842*

Armand Jacques Leroy de Saint-Arnaud (1801-1854) spent an adventurous youth in the army under the Restoration and as a soldier of fortune in Greece and elsewhere in the Mediterranean area until he made a name for himself in Algeria. He became a general in 1847, helped with Louis Napoleon's coup of 1851, became a Marshal of France, and commanded French forces in the Crimea.

✓   ✓   ✓

At the bivouac of Sidi-Ali-Ben-Rabbah, on the Narh-Ouassel, desert of Angad, October 31, 1842

Although very far from Milianah, dear Brother, I must go back there to take up our point of departure and tell you all about my operations. Take your map. I have mine before me.

Left Milianah the 26th, to go to the aid of the Aga of the Ouled-Aïad and try to lay my hands on the retinue of Ben-Allal. It was urgent, and the distance usually done in four days, I have covered in three. . . . Well, Brother, I left this point

* Lettres du maréchal de Saint-Arnaud. Vol. I, Paris, 1855, pp. 436-439, abridged.

the 28th, at six o'clock in the evening, with 400 infantrymen without packs, 80 horses and a contingent of 800 Arab horsemen drawn by the lure of pillaging. At daybreak, I was at Tissumsily; I had marched 12 hours and covered 12 leagues. There, I placed my infantry and my two howitzers on the heights, with orders to follow my movements as much as possible, while guarding always the highest points, so as to be in view of the enemy and impress him.

These dispositions taken, I put forth my enormous contingent in a line, a magnificent sight which I will never forget. With my little troop of cavalry I supported the contingent while advancing in good order and at a quick trot. . . . In an instant this avalanche of horsemen, dispersed over more than three leagues of territory, pillaged and raided three fine rich tribes. Each group does its part, but soon the scene changes. The enemy horsemen, furious at seeing their huts burned, their women abducted, their flocks stolen, turn round, charge my contingent, and drive it back pell-mell. I had foreseen this: my role was commencing. I leave a platoon in reserve, and with the three others I make an all-out assault on the enemy. Oh! Brother, I knew then that I was born to be a cavalry officer. At the first shot my whole Arab contingent, except for the three Agas, gave ground and made off with its booty. I found myself all tangled with the enemy, but not for long. My fearless cavalry scattered this band of Bedouins—we pursued them for an hour and a half. . . . My lucky star served me there as elsewhere. A decent enemy Arab, whom I took for a friend and who galloped at my side, shot at me at point blank range. He really singed me, and the shock was so great, that I was left giddy. My horse's mane was burned, but neither he nor I had a scratch. That Arab was killed five paces farther by my orderly officer, M. Martin, who received a saber blow that cut his cap and entered the leather, a trifle. Now, let us see the result: as the Arabs themselves admit, I have taken 150 camels, 500 oxen and 5000 sheep, an enormous number of mules and oxen loaded with tents, and 100 prisoners. Well, from all that, do you know what I have taken back to my bivouac? Four thousand sheep. Our cowards, our pillagers of friends, had left us to face the enemy fire and had profited from our advanced position to flee in the opposite direction. Their objective was accomplished; mine also, for I would have distributed the camels to them; therefore, they only took from me the pleasure of giving. The fact is, I ruined our enemies and enriched our so-called friends. The Aga of the south is in ecstasy; his enemies will come no more to harass him. . . . Near today's bivouac there is on the summit of a mountain a marabout ruin. Someone climbed up there and carved on a stone: Column from Milianah, COLONEL SAINT-ARNAUD, 6th *battalion of Orleans,* 53rd, 58th, 64th of the *line,* 4th *light cavalry,* 31 *October* 1842. There it is for the curious to see. . . .

— Reading No. 26 —

GENERAL BUGEAUD ON ALGERIA, 1848*

Thomas Robert Bugeaud de la Piconnerie (1784-1849) was a noble and a Napoleonic veteran who had been forced into retirement under the Restoration. The July Monarchy revived his military career, and it was he who conquered most of Algeria in the 1840's and became governor there. He was also a deputy.

To General Charon.

La Durantie, Sept. 4, 1848.

My dear General,

. . . I am familiar with the way in which you fulfill your duties; . . . there is always work to do when it is a question of Algeria. It is a country which has used up many men, materially and morally. It will still use very many more of them as well as plenty of money. God grant that it may not be unproductive, as in the past! This unfruitfulness of results other than those of conquest results from the absence of true ideas on the part of the immense majority of the ruling groups. . . . They wanted to play at colonization and civilization in flower pots, on the terraces of Algiers. When the country had been subdued, conquered against their advice and their predictions, their unreasonable demands became so inflated that they asked us to do the work of centuries in one or two years. We had to improvise a vast colonization with very little money and with the scum of all the peoples who border the Mediterranean.

* *Lettres inédites du Maréchal Bugeaud, duc d'Isly (1808-1849).* Paris, Émile-Paul Frères, 1923, pp. 323-325, abridged. Reprinted by permission of the publishers.

It is true that some writers gave us very simple means of effecting these wonders. There was needed only a very small law with three articles: 1. Algeria is joined to France; 2. Algeria is divided into departments and *arrondissements;* 3. each *arrondissement* sends a deputy to the Chamber. . . .

Ah well! Algeria has been given all that, except assimilation. Do you see any miracle yet? The money is gone and the population, instead of coming in floods, departs every day, in spite of these precious liberties. Liberties are a good thing, when one has enough to eat well, when one is well-housed and well-clothed, and when one has the assurance that all this will last. But liberty does not provide all that; it has to be obtained by very hard, very persevering work, and you also need enough capital to reclaim the land, that great tool of work. It is necessary to construct a house and sheds; it is necessary to buy livestock, agricultural tools, seed, house furnishings, and finally it is necessary to guarantee subsistence until the land can provide it. . . .

I see with pleasure that at last public opinion is won over to an idea that I have set forth for some time, that of sending to Algeria the overflow of the population of our cities, and even transported convicts. This would with a single blow attain several great ends: 1. rid France of a persistently troublemaking element; 2. fulfill for a great number of proletarians a part of the absurd promises that the February Revolution made to them; 3. people the colony.

This population will be far from the equal of my military colonists; but in the present state of France, it is necessary to give up this excellent element; it is absolutely urgent to resign oneself, and at any cost, to establish in Africa those most excellent proletarians whose heads have been stuffed with the most disastrous ideas for them and for us.

FLORA TRISTAN: WOMEN OF THE WORKING CLASSES, 1843*

Flora Tristan (1803-1844), the prophetic reformer whose grandson was to be the painter Paul Gauguin, linked together two causes—the emancipation of women and the securing of social justice for wage earners.

✓　　　　　✓　　　　　✓

. . . In the life of the workers the woman is everything. She is their sole providence. If she fails them, everything fails them. . . . Yet what education, what instruction, what guidance, what moral or physical development does the woman of the people receive? None. As a child, she is left at the mercy of a mother and grandmother who themselves never received any education: the one, according to her disposition, will be brutal and ill-natured, will beat her and maltreat her without motive; the other will be feebly indifferent, and will let her do as she pleases. (In this, as in everything that I set forth, I speak in general; of course, I agree to numerous exceptions.). . . .

Instead of being sent to school, she will be kept home, in preference to her brothers, because she is more readily utilized in the household, for rocking babies, doing errands, watching over the soup, etc. At 12 she is apprenticed: there she continues to be exploited by the employer and is often as maltreated as she was by her parents. . . .

. . . Such will be the ordinary state of affairs of the poor young girl at 20. Then she will marry, without love, but only because one must marry if one wishes to escape the tyranny of the parents. What will happen to her? I imagine that she will have five children; in her turn, she will be completely incapable of raising her sons and her daughters decently; she will prove to be as brutal toward her children as her mother and grandmother were to her. . . .* . . . .

Poor workwomen! They have so many causes for irritation! First the husband. One must admit, there are few workers'

* Mme. Flora Tristan, *Union Ouvrière*. Paris, 1843, pp. 51-63, abridged.

households that are happy. The husband, having received more training, being *the head by reason of the law,* and also *by reason of the money* which he brings to the household, thinks himself (and he is in fact) very superior to the wife, who brings in only her paltry day's wages, and is, in the home, only the very humble servant.

Therefore, the husband treats his wife at the least with a great deal of disdain. The poor wife, who feels herself humiliated in every word, every look that her husband gives her, revolts openly or secretly, according to her nature; from that come violent, painful scenes, which end by causing a constant state of irritation between the *master* and the *servant* (one can even say *slave,* for the woman is, so to speak, the *property* of the husband). This state becomes so distressing, that the husband, instead of staying home to chat with his wife, hastens to flee, and as he has no other place to go, he goes to the cabaret to drink *blue wine* with *other husbands* who are not any happier than he, in the hope of *diverting his thoughts.*†. . .

After the bitter sorrows caused by the husband, next come pregnancies, illnesses, lack of work and poverty, poverty which is always planted there at the door like the head of Medusa. Add to all that the incessant irritation caused by four or five

---

* The women of the people prove very tender mothers to little children until they have reached the age of two or three years. The womanly instinct makes them understand that the child, during its first two years, needs continual care. But past that age, they brutalize them (save for exceptions).

† Why do the workers go to the cabaret? Egoism has struck the upper classes, those who govern, with complete blindness. They do not understand that their fate, their welfare, and their *safety* depend on the moral, intellectual, and material amelioration of the working class. They abandon the worker to poverty and ignorance, thinking according to the ancient maxim that the more the people are *brutes,* the more easily they can be *muzzled.* All this was fine before the *Declaration of the Rights of Man.* . . . Besides, one should be at least logical: if one believes that it is a good and wise policy to leave the poor in a condition of *brutality,* then why complain endlessly of their vices? . . .

In the present state of affairs, the cabaret is the TEMPLE of the worker; it is the *only place* where he can go. The Church—he doesn't believe in it; the Theater—he doesn't understand it at all. That is why the cabarets *are always full.* . . .

crying, unruly, annoying children, who turn round and round the mother, and that in a small room, where there is no space to stir. Oh! one would have to be an angel descended to earth, not to become irritated, brutal, and ill-tempered in such a position. However, in the midst of such a family, what becomes of the children? They see their father only evenings and Sundays. This father, forever in a state of irritation or drunkenness, speaks to them only in anger, and they receive from him only insults and blows; hearing their mother continually complaining about him, they learn to feel hate and scorn for him. As for their mother, they fear her, obey her, but do not love her. . . . Having no attraction in the vicinity of the mother, the child will seek any pretext to escape from the maternal household. Bad associations are easy to make, for girls as for boys. . . .

I repeat: the woman is everything in the life of the worker. . . .

Do you begin to understand, you men who cry shame without stopping to examine the question, why I claim *rights for women?* . . .

. . . All the evils of the working class are summed up by these two words: poverty and ignorance, ignorance and poverty. But, in order to get out of this labyrinth, I see only one way: *begin by educating the women, because the women are in charge of raising the children, male and female.* . . .

— Reading No. 28 —

FLORA TRISTAN: "UNION OUVRIÈRE," 1843 *

What is the objective and what will be the result of the *universal union* of workmen and workwomen?

It has as objectives:

1. To *form* the compact, indissoluble *unity* of the *working class;*

* Mme. Flora Tristan, *Union Ouvrière*. Paris, 1843, pp. 17-28, abridged.

2. To make the *Workers' Union* the possessor of an enormous capital, by means of a voluntary contribution from each worker;

3. To acquire, by means of this capital, some real power, that of money;

4. By means of this power, to prevent poverty and to eradicate the evil at its root, in giving children of the working class a solid, rational education, capable of making them into trained, reasonable, intelligent men and women who are also skillful in their professions;

5. To compensate all sorts of labor amply and worthily.

This is too beautiful! someone will cry. It is too beautiful: or, *it is impossible.*

Readers, before paralyzing the impulses of your heart and imagination by this glacial phrase, *it is impossible,* always keep in mind that France contains seven to eight million workers; that, at two francs apiece, makes at the end of the year 14 million; at four francs, 28 million; at eight francs, 56 million. . . .

. . . I have said that by means of this capital, the *Workers' Union* could gain real power, that which money gives. Let us see how:

For example the Irish people by means of their union, have been able to establish and maintain what is called the *Association;* moreover it has been able to set up, by voluntary contribution . . . a colossal fortune for a man of heart and talent, O'Connell. . . .

What is the social position of the working class in France today, and what rights remain for it to claim? . . .

In reading the Charter of 1830, one is struck by a serious omission. . . . Our constitutional legislators have forgotten that prior to the Rights of Man and Citizen, there exists an imperious, imprescriptible right which precedes and dominates all the others, *the right to live.* Now, for the poor worker who possesses neither land nor houses, nor capital, nor absolutely anything except *his arms,* the Rights of Man and Citizen are of no value (and in this case they even become for him a bitter mockery), if first one does not recognize *his right to live,* and, for the worker, the right to live is *the right to work,* the *only one* which can give him the possibility of *eating,* and consequently of living. . . .

The working class has, then, two important claims to make: 1. *The Right to Work;* 2. *The Organization of Labor.*

But, someone is going to say again, what you demand for the working class is *impossible.* The right to work! They won't get it. This claim, however just and legal, will be considered as an attack on property properly so-called (land, houses, capital), and the organization of labor will be considered as an attack on the rights of free competition; now, since those who manage the governmental machine are the owners of land and capital, it is evident that they will never consent to grant equal rights to the working class. . . .

Workers, you see the situation. If you want to save yourselves, you have only one means: you must *unite*. . . .

Since '89 the bourgeois class IS CONSTITUTED. Notice what force a body united by the same interests can have. . . .

This bourgeois-proprietor class *represents itself* in the Chamber and before the nation, not in order to *defend its interests* there, for no one threatens them, but in order to *impose* its conditions on the 25 million proletarians, its subordinates. In a word, it makes itself *judge* and *party,* absolutely as the feudal lords behaved whom it has overthrown. . . .

You see, the *noble class* has been succeeded by the *bourgeois class,* already much *more numerous* and *more useful;* it now remains to CONSTITUTE THE WORKING CLASS. It is necessary, then, that the workers, the enduring part of the nation, in their turn form a vast UNION AND ESTABLISH THEMSELVES IN UNITY! Oh, then the working class will be strong; then it will be able to demand of the bourgeois both its RIGHT TO WORK and the ORGANIZATION OF LABOR; and make itself be listened to. . . .

— Reading No. 29 —

THIERS-GUIZOT DEBATE ON PAST AND PRESENT POLITICS, 1846*

Thiers rises to object to remarks about him by Guizot in a previous debate and, after discussing various governmental policies, reaches the constitutional question. After his conclusion, Guizot responds.

✓   ✓   ✓

* *Annales du parlement français, publiées . . . sous la direction de M. T. Fleury.* Vol. VIII, Paris, 1847, pp. 905-913.

Chamber of Deputies
May 29, 1846

M. Thiers:

. . . What have I done? . . . I have merely presented the English theory. . . . It is true that in presenting this picture, an oft repeated objection suddenly came to my mind. I had often heard it said, not in the tribune, but privately: . . . France is not constituted in the same manner as England; she cannot accept representative government in its full sense. . . . Then, unable to master a sudden emotion . . . I cried: We should have been told that in 1830. . . .

I have not wished, to any degree whatever, . . . to disturb the contract of 1830. . . .

. . . I am profoundly a monarchist. I believe that when a state, a great state, does not have a king it soon makes one. . . . A king is . . . provided in order not to have a usurper.

But enlightened nations cannot be governed like the states of Asia. It has been necessary to guard against the inconveniences of heredity. . . . Now, to correct this inconvenience a system as wise as it is simple was invented, which consists, in all of our representative constitutions, of placing beside this king men who are seriously responsible, that is, men having the reality and the appearance of power. . . .

That, gentlemen, is what I was brought up to believe. . . .

But the spectacle which we witnessed under the Restoration imprinted these ideas, in a manner of speaking, all the more deeply in our minds. . . .

The prince who last reigned in France, Charles X, had estimable qualities; he was honest, religious, generous; but, as you know, he had a passion for interfering in government. You know that he had it to such a point that even when he was only the brother of the king he wished to govern.

When he was king it was even more the case. (Smiles.) He had unfortunate prejudices: he was religious, honest, and good, as I said; but, having lived in the revolution, every time that liberty in the shape of representative institutions, even wise and moderate ones, appeared before him, he believed that it was the revolution, and that if he yielded he would go to the scaffold like Louis XVI.

He was obsessed by this idea, and in order to be true to it he intervened ardently in the government. . . .

When the Martignac ministry was formed, this king, considering himself defeated, was constantly malevolent, not against persons—his nature was excellent—but against the system . . . and finally on a day of towering rage cried 'No more concessions!' (Movement.)

No more concessions! . . . May God preserve me from

wishing to draw sinister forecasts from this. Oh no! . . . I
believe that France will in future correct solely by electoral
movements what she was formerly obliged to correct by revolution. (Assent on the left. Murmurs in the center.)

We who have witnessed this spectacle, we emerged from the
Restoration full of this conviction, that royalty must never be
compromised in the government's battles; that it must in these
affairs be as little visible as possible; convinced that representative government is the more real and the more true when
there are, at the side of royalty, ministers who are more seriously responsible, that is, more truly exercising the power.

On this point I know that there are differences of degree
. . . but it will not be disputed that, in the view of all men
who are reasonable—really monarchist and constitutionalist—
the system is the more true when the ministers . . . do not
efface themselves, . . . do not consent to the role of mere in-
termediaries between the powers. . . .

M. Guizot:

. . . The honorable previous speaker attacked us as follows:
'The policy which you carry out is not your own; you are only
the instruments . . . of the influence which wills this policy;
if I had wished to do as you have done, I would have remained
a minister.'

There is the meaning; there, I believe, are the very words of
the honorable previous speaker. . . .

I myself proclaimed yesterday your right, the most delicate,
the most perilous of all, the right to say that the influence of
the crown was excessive, and to argue for this view; I recognized your right; but against whom should you complain in
exercising this right? Against the cabinet alone. . . .

I have something else to dispose of, something, the honorable
M. Thiers will permit me to say to him, which was not happily
phrased in what he said a while ago from this tribune; it is the
example of the unfortunate King Charles X. It is very true that
it was for not having understood that representative government requires the accord of the powers, . . . that Charles X
fell.

I do not think that anyone supposes that this truth is not
understood and would not be constantly accepted today. (Very
good!) . . .

The comparison is thus not a happy one. . . .

Here is the difference between the honorable M. Thiers and
me.

My conviction is that the men to whom the crown does the
honor of taking them for councilors and to whom the Chambers
do the honor of giving them the majority, that these men are
called upon to govern and to maintain the accord and union

between the powers, a necessary and fundamental condition of representative government. . . .

It is labor for the ministers to prove constantly to the Chambers that they [*the ministers*] are right. . . .

. . . I add that it is their duty to perform the same labor with respect to the crown.

The crown is not, whatever the honorable previous speaker may have appeared to say about it . . . the crown is not an armchair which has been locked up so that no one may sit there, and solely to prevent usurpation, as you put it a while ago. That is not true: the crown is also something else; the crown is necessary, the monarchy is necessary, not merely to prevent usurpation, to halt the ambitious, but as an active and real part of the government. . . .

An intelligent, free person, who has his own ideas, sentiments, and desires, like all real and living beings, sits in this armchair. The duty of this royal person . . . is to govern only in accord with the great public powers instituted by the Charter, with their assent, their adhesion, their support. This is the duty to which Charles X failed.

There will be no repetition of this failure among us.

Today the duty of the councilors of the crown is to see that the same ideas, the same measures, and the same policy which they are able to make prevail in the Chambers prevails with respect to the crown.

There you have constitutional government; . . . we must all have for the crown . . . this respect which amounts to believing that it is worn by an intelligent and free being, with whom we treat, and not by a pure machine . . . made to occupy a place which others would take if it were not there. . . .

(*Voice from the left:* And the Queen of England!)

If the honorable members who interrupt me knew to what extent the ideas and the sentiments which I express at this moment are present and familiar to all the minds in England (Movement); if they knew to what degree the greatest, the most independent, the proudest ministers who ever governed in England, have taken account, on the greatest of occasions, of the ideas, sentiments, and opinions of the crown. . . .

GUIZOT ON SUFFRAGE AND POLITICAL CAPACITY, 1847*

Guizot here debates against a proposal in March, 1847, by Duvergier de Hauranne (see Reading No. 32) for a slight lowering of the property qualification for eligibility to vote and for the extension of the suffrage to persons of proved intellectual capacity.

✓   ✓   ✓

Chamber of Deputies
March 26, 1847

. . . France from 1789 to 1817 was continually trying either to realize or to avoid, I shall not say the principle of universal suffrage: the principle of universal suffrage is in itself so absurd that not one of its partisans even dares to accept it and uphold it in its entirety. (Expressions of denial on the extreme left.) Not one. (M. Garnier-Pagès: Its day will come.) There is no day for universal suffrage. There is no day when all human creatures whoever they are can be called to exercise political rights. . . .

The electoral law of 1817 was the first to have the courage to reject this principle absolutely, to cease locating the electoral right in numbers and to proclaim that the right belonged to political capacity. At the same time the law located political capacity in a certain social situation based on industrial or landed property.

There you have the principle which was introduced into our public law in 1817, a principle which has removed political power from the region of numbers to place it in elevated and stable regions where the real awareness of the great interests of the social order is to be found. That was more than a reform; that was a real and salutary revolution, in our ideas, in our political institutions. . . .

The 1817 legislation, in the first place, adopted direct election. . . . the only kind which really links the electors to the elected. (That's true!) It did more. . . . Our electoral system

---

* *Annales du parlement français. . . .* Vol. IX, Paris, 1848, pp. 299-301.

. . . judged that the election . . . should be linked to the whole existence of the electors, to their habitual relations; that it should bring together, for the electoral operation, the men who were accustomed to living together, who had interests in common, who really knew each other; it accepted natural groups of electors such as are to be found either in territorial divisions, affinities of interests, or real and practical circumstances; it took them and had them do the electing; to each natural group, its deputy.

These, then, are the two essential principles on which our electoral system rests: political capacity, and legal adoption of natural groups of electors. . . .

There is a great difference between political and purely intellectual capacity. When political capacity was attached to a certain property, it was done, in the first place, with the presumption that intelligence was indeed there; but there was also the presumption that the intelligence which was there was one which was enlightened by its situation concerning the true and essential interests of the social order. (Very good!)

There you have the meaning of political capacity in our present electoral system.

Gentlemen, I have infinite respect for intelligence. . . . But I do not entrust myself blindly to intelligence. . . . Excessive confidence in human intelligence, human pride, pride of the spirit—permit me to call things by their right names—has been the malady of our times, (Movement) the cause of a great part of our errors and our ills. Intelligence, as I had the honor to say to the Chamber a while back, needs to be ceaselessly cautioned, contained, enlightened, guided by the social situation. The honorable M. Duvergier de Hauranne today treats intelligence in the way the nobility were treated in former times: they were asked what they were, whether they were nobles, and then they were asked nothing further. (Laughs of approbation.)

Well, I believe that that was a mistake and that it would be just as much a mistake today; like the nobility, intelligence . . . must be required to meet certain conditions, . . . to give certain guarantees of its rectitude, of its fidelity to the great principles of the social order. That is what our electoral system demands of it, nothing more and nothing less. (Very good!). . . .

LOUIS BLANC: RIGHTS, LIBERTY, AND SOCIAL REFORM, 1847*

Louis Blanc's Organisation du travail *first appeared in 1839. This introduction to the fifth edition is dated July, 1847. The passage quoted should help place its author in relation to socialist and democratic tendencies on the eve of the 1848 revolution.*

✦   ✦   ✦

. . . But does not the poor man have a *right* to better himself? Yet what does it matter, if he lacks the *power?* What good is the *right* to be cured to the invalid whom no one cures?

Rights, considered in an abstract manner, are the mirage which, since 1789, has deluded the people. Rights are a dead, metaphysical protection which has replaced, for the people, the living protection owed to them. Rights, pompously and with no results proclaimed in charters, have served only to mask the injustice of a regime of individualism and the barbarism of the abandonment of the poor. It is because liberty has been defined with the word *right* that men have been called free who were slaves to hunger, slaves to cold, slaves to ignorance, slaves to chance. Let us then say once and for all: liberty consists not only in a RIGHT granted but in the POWER given to a man to exercise, to develop his faculties under the empire of justice and under the safeguards of the law.

And note well, this is not a futile distinction: its meaning is profound; its consequences are immense. For as soon as one admits that man needs, to be truly free, the *power* to exercise and develop his faculties, it follows that society owes to each of its members both the education, without which the human understanding *cannot* develop, and the instruments of labor, without which human *activity* cannot be given free scope. Now by whose intervention other than the state's can society give to

* Louis Blanc, *Organisation du Travail. Cinquième édition.* Paris, 1948. "Introduction" (dated *Juillet,* 1847), reprinted in J. A. R. Marriott, ed., *The French Revolution of 1848 in Its Economic Aspect.* Vol. I, Oxford, Clarendon Press, 1913, pp. 19-20. Reprinted by permission of Oxford University Press.

each of its members suitable instruction and the tools necessary for work? Thus it is in the name, and for the sake, of liberty that we demand the rehabilitation of the principle of authority. We want a strong government because, in the regime of inequality in which we are still vegetating there are feeble persons who need a social force to protect them. We want a government which intervenes in industry because in a situation where loans are made only to the rich there is need of a social banker who will lend to the poor. In a word, we invoke the idea of the state because the liberty of the future must be real liberty.

Let there be no mistake, moreover; this need for government intervention is a relative matter; it stems only from the condition of weakness, poverty, and ignorance into which past tyrannies have plunged the people. There will come a day, if our dearest hopes are not disappointed, when there will no longer be any need for a strong and active government, because there will no longer be in society any inferior class in a state of minority. Until then, the establishment of a tutelary authority is indispensable. Socialism can be fertilized only by politics.

Oh rich people, you are being deceived when you are turned against those who are devoting themselves to the calm and pacific solution of social problems. Yes, this holy cause of the poor is your cause. A solidarity of heavenly origin binds you to their poverty by fear, and links you by your very self-interest to their future deliverance. . . .

— Reading No. 32 —

BANQUET SPEECH OF M. DUVERGIER DE HAURANNE, 1847*

Prosper Duvergier de Hauranne (1798-1881) was a loyal Orleanist deputy but a member of the dynastic opposition after

* Discours de M. Duvergier de Hauranne, député du Cher, Au Banquet réformiste de la Nièvre. Tenu à la Charité-sur-Loire le 17 Octobre 1847. Nevers, 1847, pp. 3-11, abridged.

1837. In Des principes du gouvernement représentatif et de leur application *(1838) he formulated the celebrated phrase, "The King reigns and does not govern." It was his modest proposal for parliamentary reform in March, 1847, which was opposed by Guizot in a famous speech (see Reading No. 30). Under the Second Empire his* Histoire du gouvernement parlementaire en France *(10 vols., 1857-1872) was to help keep alive the idea of parliamentary government.*

$$✓ \qquad ✓ \qquad ✓$$

Last winter when I submitted an electoral reform project to the Chamber, Messieurs the ministers of Interior and Foreign Affairs. . . . claimed that it was just a whim (Laughter) . . . with no relation to any of the wishes or needs of the country. What do they have to say about this now? Do they think that a little whim has been able to convoke these numerous and imposing assemblies which from one end of France to the other give rise to the same cry? (No, no!). . .

. . . In 1846, when we uttered the word, the vile word "corruption" (Laughter), there was no lack of people to tell us that it was a ridiculous phantom evoked by personal ambitions. . . . Today there are still, I know, a few persons who deny the corruption. Is there anyone here who doesn't believe it? (No, no. Applause.). . .

But if the methods of the present government are detestable, are the accomplishments any better? . . .

Does it seem to you . . . that the Spanish double marriage, that great stroke of current policy, has added much to the glory, to the grandeur of our country? (No, no! France is dishonored.) . . .

In your opinion was all that worth the sacrifice of Cracow . . . ? (No, no.)

Do you think that it is honest, just, statesmanlike to take sides in Switzerland with the ultramontane minority against the liberal majority, to give or sell arms to this minority and to refuse an allied state the right which all independent states have, that of reforming its own constitution? (No, no.)

Do you take pleasure in watching the government of France set obstacles in the way of . . . the great pontiff who wishes to re-establish in the world the alliance of religion and liberty? (No, no! *Vive* Pius IX!)

Finally, do you find it good that after having sacrificed the honor and interests of France to England for five years, today they sacrifice to Austria the great cause of the liberty of peoples and of European civilization? (No, no.) . . . .

Are you satisfied . . . with the condition of your finances (no), and do you approve of a system which . . . has added . . . new and bigger deficits? (Prolonged movement.)

Representative government corrupted in its principles, falsified in its mechanism, perverted in its consequences, the public morals enfeebled and poisoned, the great national interests in foreign and domestic affairs sacrificed to miserable political combinations, or to family interests (Lively applause), that is what we witness 17 years after the July Revolution, seven years after the formation of the present ministry: do you want that to continue? (No, no. Prolonged movement.) Well, if you don't like it, help us to put an end to it (Yes, yes, we'll help you), and to do that, pending the elections, sign and get others to sign the reform petition. (We'll sign. *Vive la Réforme!*) . . . .

. . . As matters stand, it's a question of knowing whether representative government was created so that 459 deputies and 230,000 electors can quietly carry on their private affairs and those of their families at the expense of the country. (Yes, yes. Bravo!) It's a question of whether constitutional monarchy, that admirable compromise between absolute monarchy and a republic, will perish, exhausted, enervated, rebuked, in the shameful embraces of those who seek in her only the satisfying of their brutal passion for money and power. (Prolonged movement. Lively applause.) It's a question, in a word, of knowing whether we shall be able by legal and moderate remedies to prevent in time the always fearful recourse to violent and irregular means.

So, Gentlemen, *to electoral and parliamentary reform,* because this reform is just, statesmanlike, and opportune! (Bravo!) . . . .

To electoral and parliamentary reform, because wise reforms prevent revolutions. (Prolonged movement. Thunder of applause. *Vive la réforme! Vive* M. Duvergier de Hauranne!). . . .

— Reading No. 33 —

ALEXIS DE TOCQUEVILLE: SPEECH TO THE CHAMBER OF DEPUTIES, JANUARY 27, 1848*

Chamber of Deputies
January 27, 1848

. . . If I cast an attentive glance at the governing class . . . and on that which is governed, what is taking place frightens and disturbs me. And to speak first of what I have called the class which governs—and note well that I do not compose this class uniquely of what these days has been improperly called the middle class, but of all those in whatever position who enjoy political rights . . . —I say that what exists in this class disturbs and frightens me. What I see, Gentlemen, I can express it with a word: the public moral standards are changing . . . ; more and more in place of generally accepted opinions, sentiments, and ideas one sees individual interests, individual aims, and attitudes borrowed from private life and private interests. . . .

France was first to give the world in the midst of the crashing and thunder of its first revolution principles which since have been found to be regenerative principles of all human societies. That was its glory. . . . Well, those are the principles which our example is enfeebling today . . . Europe, which is watching us, is beginning to wonder whether we were right or wrong . . . whether, indeed, as we have so often repeated, we are guiding human societies toward a happier and more prosperous future, or whether we are drawing them after us toward moral bankruptcy and ruin. . . .

Gentlemen, if the spectacle which we are producing has such an effect when seen from afar, from the outer edges of Europe, what effect do you think it is having in France itself upon the classes which have no rights and who, in the midst of the political incapacity to which our laws condemn them watch us acting alone in the great theater where we find ourselves! . . .

As for me, I am alarmed. It is said that there is no danger

* *Annales du parlement français publiée . . . sous la direction de M. T. Fleury.* Vol. X, Paris, 1849, pp. 106-109, slightly abridged.

because there is no insurrection; it is said that because there is no material disorder at the surface of society, we are far from revolution.

Gentlemen, permit me to say to you with complete sincerity that I believe that you are mistaken. Without doubt the disorder is not visible but it has entered profoundly into people's minds. Look at what is happening among the working classes who at present, I admit, are tranquil. It is true that they are not tormented by political passions as such, to the same degree as they formerly were; but do you not see that their passions, from political, have become social? Do you not see that there are spreading bit by bit in their midst opinions and ideas which are not aimed at overturning this or that law, ministry, or government, but society itself, at shaking it off of the bases on which it rests today? Do you not see that bit by bit it is being said among them that everything located above them is incapable and unworthy of governing them; that the distribution of property made until now in the world is unjust; that property rests on bases which are not equitable? And do you not believe that when such opinions take root, when they spread in an almost general manner, when they descend deeply into the masses, they bring sooner or later, I do not know when or how, but they bring sooner or later the most fearful revolutions?

Such, Gentlemen, is my profound conviction. I believe that at this moment we are sleeping on a volcano (Protests); I am profoundly convinced of it. (Murmurs) . . . .

When I examine what at various times, in various periods, among different peoples has been the effective cause of the downfall of governing classes, I note this or that event, man, or accidental or superficial cause; but believe me, the real reason, the effective reason which causes men to lose political power is that they have become unworthy of keeping it.

Think, Gentlemen, of the old monarchy. It was stronger than you are, stronger in its origin; it was more firmly based than you are upon ancient customs, moral standards, beliefs; it was stronger than you are, and yet it has fallen into the dust. And why did it fall? Do you think it was by some accident? Do you think it was by the act of some man, by the deficit, the oath of the Tennis Court, Lafayette, Mirabeau? No, Gentlemen, there is a deeper and truer reason. The class which was governing then had beome, through its indifference, its egoism, and its vices, incapable and unworthy of governing. (Very good!)

There you have the true reason.

Well, Gentlemen . . . do you not feel . . . that the earth is quaking once again in Europe? (Movement.) Do you not feel . . . a wind of revolution in the air? This wind, no one knows where it comes from, where it blows, or, believe me, whom it will carry with it; and it is in such times that you remain calm in the presence of the degradation of public morality—for the term is not too strong.

I speak here without bitterness; I speak to you, I believe, even without any party spirit; I am attacking men against whom I feel no vindictiveness; but for all that I must express to my antagonists and to my country my firm and profound conviction. Well, then, my firm and profound conviction is this: that public morality is being degraded, and that the degradation of public morality will shortly, very shortly perhaps, lead you into new revolutions. . . .

Legislative changes have been mentioned. I am very much inclined to think that these changes are not only useful, but necessary: thus I believe in the need for electoral reform; but I am not so mad, Gentlemen, as to fail to see that it is not by laws alone, which are, in the last analysis, only the details of the business; no, it is not the mechanism of the laws which produces great events; what produces these events, Gentlemen, is the inner spirit of the government. Keep the laws as they are, if you wish. I think you would be very wrong to do so, but keep them. Keep the men too, if it gives you any pleasure; I raise no objection. But in God's name change the spirit of the government; for, I repeat, that spirit is leading you to the abyss. (Lively approbation from the left.)

— Reading No. 34 —

THE LAST MEETING OF THE CHAMBER OF DEPUTIES, FEBRUARY 24, 1848 *

This remarkable document was produced by the indomitable stenographers of the Moniteur *who refused to let drama or disorder stay their pens.*

* Moniteur officiel, of Feb. 25, 1848. Reprinted in J. B. Duvergier, Collection complète des lois . . . Vol. 48, année 1848, pp. 49-57, abridged.

Where substantial abridgements have been made, bracketed explanations have been supplied by the translator.

✐ ✐ ✐

Chamber of Deputies. Chairmanship, M. Sauzet. Session of Thursday 24 February. (*Moniteur du 25.*)

The Chamber was convoked for today at one o'clock . . . but the deputies crowd into the hall and summon the president, who, at 12:30, comes to take the chair. . . .

Violent agitation reigns in the Assembly. . . . The rumor gains ground of the king's abdication in favor of the Count of Paris, under the regency of Madame the Duchess of Orleans.

At 1:30, it is announced that Madame the Duchess of Orleans and M. the Count of Paris are going to attend the session.

At the same instant, in fact, Madame the Duchess of Orleans enters, holding M. the Count of Paris by one hand and M. the Duke of Chartres by the other. Lively applause welcomes her. . . .

Madame the Duchess of Orleans and her children sit on seats that have been hastily placed in the hemicycle, at the foot of the rostrum. M. the Duke of Nemours accompanies the Duchess of Orleans. Several officers and national guardsmen in uniform serve her as an escort.

A certain number of people foreign to the Chamber also enter and remain standing in the two aisles.

Great anxiety shows on all faces.

M. Lacrosse, in the midst of noise. I ask that permission to speak be given to M. Dupin, who has just conducted M. the Count of Paris into the Assembly.

M. Dupin. I haven't asked for it!

Numerous voices. Speak! Speak!

M. Dupin, at the rostrum. (Listen! Listen!) Gentlemen, you know the situation in the capital, the manifestations which have taken place. They have resulted in the abdication of His Majesty Louis Philippe, who stated at that time that he was laying aside the authority and that he was leaving it for free transmission to the Count of Paris with the regency of Madame the Duchess of Orleans. (Lively acclamations. . . .)

Gentlemen, your acclamations, so precious for the new king and for Madame the Regent, are not the first which have greeted her; she crossed the Tuileries and the Place de la Concorde on foot, escorted by the people, by the National Guard (Bravo! bravo!) . . . .

M. Dupin leaves the rostrum. . . .

[*There follows much discussion of whether the Chamber can deliberate in the presence of the Duchess of Orleans and the*

Count of Paris. Disorder mounts as strangers enter and refuse to leave when ordered to do so. There are objections to the regency and demands for a provisional government, and even for a constituent Assembly.]

M. *Odilon Barrot*. (Listen! Listen!) Never have we greater need for self-control and prudence! (It's true!) May you all be united in the same sentiment: that of saving the country from the most detestable of calamities, civil war. (Very good! Very good!) Nations do not die; but they can be weakened by internal dissensions, and never has France had a greater need for all its grandeur and all its strength.

Our duty is clear. . . .

The crown of July rests on the head of a child and on that of a woman. (Lively acclamations in the center.)

(Madame the Duchess of Orleans gets up and salutes the Assembly. She calls upon the Count of Paris to imitate her, which he does.)

M. *Odilon Barrot*. I make a solemn appeal. . . .

M. *de la Rochejaquelein*. You don't know what you are doing!

(Madame the Duchess of Orleans gets up as if to speak.)

Several voices. Listen! Listen! Let Madame the Duchess speak!

Other members. Continue, M. Barrot!

M. *Odilon Barrot*. It is in the name of political liberty in our country, it is in the name of the need for order above all, in the name of our unity and agreement in such difficult circumstances, that I ask my whole country to rally around its representatives, its July Revolution. . . . (Bravos in the center.)

M. *de la Rochejaquelein*. I demand permission to speak.

M. *Odilon Barrot*. Is there by chance a pretension to call into question what we decided by the July Revolution? (Very good! Very good!)

Gentlemen, the circumstances are difficult, I agree; but there are in this country such elements of greatness, of generosity, and of good sense, that I am convinced that we need only appeal to them for the population of Paris to rally around this standard. (Yes! Yes!) . . . .

. . . The regency of the Duchess of Orleans, a ministry taken from among those with the most tested opinions, will best guarantee liberty; and may an appeal to the nation, to public opinion in all its liberty, then be pronounced, and be pronounced without going astray to the point of rival claims and civil war. . . .

M. *Ledru-Rollin*. I demand permission to speak.

M. *Barrot, continuing*. Be pronounced in the name of the interests of the country and of true liberty. . . .

[*There are more incursions, and the disorder increases. There are calls for a republic. The Duchess of Orleans and her children have disappeared. Some of the intruders take over the rostrum.*]

(MM. Crémieux, Ledru-Rollin and de Lamartine appear simultaneously at the rostrum.)

Voice from the crowd. No more Bourbons!—Down with the traitors!—A provisional government immediately!

(Confused outcries. Many deputies withdraw through the door at the back.)

M. Ledru-Rollin, addressing himself to the men in the crowd. In the name of the people whom you represent, I demand silence from you.

Voice from the people. In the name of M. Ledru-Rollin, silence!

M. Ledru-Rollin. Gentlemen, in the name of the people, I demand a moment of silence!

A man of the people. A provisional government!

M. Mauguin. Be quiet! You will have a provisional government!

M. Ledru-Rollin. In the name of the people everywhere in arms, masters of Paris whatever happens (Yes! yes!), I come to protest against the kind of government which has been proposed from this rostrum. (Very good! very good! Bravos in the crowd.) . . . [Ledru-Rollin concludes, after many interruptions.]

I demand then, in summary, a provisional government (Yes! yes!), not named by the Chamber (No! no!), but by the people; a provisional government, and an immediate call for a convention to regularize the rights of the people. (Bravo! bravo!)

(M. de Lamartine, who has stayed at the rostrum, advances to speak.)

Several voices. Lamartine! Lamartine! Applause breaks out. Listen! Listen!

M. de Lamartine. Gentlemen, I felt as deeply as any among you the double sentiment which gripped this arena a short time ago at the sight of one of the most touching spectacles presented by human annals, that of a majestic princess pleading her cause with her innocent son, and coming from a deserted palace to cast herself in the midst of the representation of the people. (Very good! very good!—Listen! listen!—We can't hear! Repeat!)

I want to repeat my sentence, and I beg you to wait for what will follow it.

I said, Gentlemen, that I had felt as deeply as anyone in this enclosure the double sentiment which agitated it a little while ago. And here I make no distinction, for the occasion does not call for it, between national representation and the representation of the citizens, of all the people, and moreover this is a time for equality, and this equality, I am sure, will only serve to secure recognition for the priority of the mission that certain men have received from their country, in order to give, not appeasement, but the first signal for the re-establishment of harmony and public peace. (Bravo! Bravo!)

But, Gentlemen, if I share the emotions inspired by this touching spectacle of the greatest of human catastrophes, if I share the respect which animates all of you here in this room, whatever your opinions, I have shared no less acutely the respect for this splendid people who have been fighting for three days to correct a perfidious government, and to re-establish on a foundation henceforth unshakable the empire of order and liberty. (Applause.)

Gentlemen, I do not share the illusion that was brought to this rostrum a while ago; I do not think that a spontaneous acclamation wrested from emotion and from public sentiment can constitute a firm and unshakable law for a government of 35 million men.

I know that what an acclamation proclaims, another acclamation can take away, and whatever the government which the wisdom and interests of this country may produce, in the present crisis it is important to the people, to all classes of the population, to those who have shed their blood in this struggle, to make of it finally a popular, solid, unshakable government. (Applause.)

Ah, well, Gentlemen, how to do it? How to find it among these shifting elements, in this tempest where we are all carried away. . . . How to find this unshakable basis, in going to the very heart of the country, to extract, as it were, the great mystery of the nation's law (Profound sensation), from which all order comes, and all truth, and all liberty.

It is for this reason that, far from having recourse to these subterfuges, to these surprises, to these emotions which a country, you see, sooner or later regrets (Yes! yes!) when these fictions come to evaporate, leaving nothing solid, permanent, truly popular, and unshakable under the tread of the country; it is for this reason that I come to support with all my might the double demand that I would have been the first to make at this rostrum, if I had been permitted at the beginning of the session, the demand, first for a government, I acknowledge of necessity, of public order, of circumstance, for a government which stanches the flow of blood, for a government which stops the civil war among its citizens. . . . (Applause.)

(One man from the crowd, who stands in the hemicycle,

puts his sword back in the scabbard, saying: "Bravo! Bravo!")

A voice. No more royalty!

M. de Lamartine. . . . For a government which stops this terrible misunderstanding which has existed for some years between the different classes of citizens, and which, in preventing our recognizing ourselves as a single people, keeps us from liking and embracing each other. (Very good! very good!)

So I demand that there be constituted immediately, in the name of the public peace, of the blood which flows, of the people . . . I demand that a provisional government be set up . . . (Bravo! bravo!), a government which prejudges nothing, neither our rights, nor our resentments, nor our sympathies, nor our angers, concerning the definitive government that the country will want to give when it shall have been consulted. (That's it! that's it!)

I demand therefore a provisional government. (Yes! yes!)

From all sides. The names of the members of the provisional government!

(Several people present a list to M. de Lamartine.)

M. de Lamartine. Wait!

This provisional government will have as its mission, its first and great mission, I maintain: 1. to establish the indispensible truce, public peace among the citizens; 2. to prepare immediately the necessary measures for convoking the entire country, and for consulting it, for consulting the whole National Guard (Yes! yes!), the whole country, all who as men bear the rights of citizens. (Prolonged applause.)

A last word.

The powers which have succeeded one another for 50 years. . . .

(At this moment, from outside are heard at the doors of one of the public galleries some violent blows resounding. The doors soon yield under the blows of the butt ends of guns. Men of the people mixed with national guardsmen come in crying: "Down with the Chamber! no deputies!" One of the men lowers the barrel of his gun in the direction of the rostrum. Cries of "Don't shoot! don't shoot! It is M. de Lamartine who is speaking!" resound loudly. On the insistence of his comrades, the man puts up his gun.)

The President, who has remained in his chair, calls for silence, waving his bell wildly.

(The noise and the tumult gain in intensity.)

The President. Since I cannot obtain silence, I declare the session closed.

(M. Sauzet leaves the chair after having uttered these words.)

Here the meeting of the Chamber of Deputies ends; but the people, armed with guns and swords, mixed with national guardsmen and a certain number of deputies, chiefly deputies of the Left, remain in the room. . . .

[*As the disorderly meeting continues, Lamartine and Dupont de l'Eure attempt to read the names of a provisional government.*]

A citizen. It is necessary that the members of the provisional government shout: *Long live the Republic!* before being nominated and accepted.

Another. I demand the dismissal of all the absent deputies.

Another. It is necessary to take the provisional government to the City Hall. We want a wise, moderate, government! No blood! But we want a republic!

M. Bocage. To the City Hall, Lamartine leading!

(M. de Lamartine leaves the Chamber accompanied by a great number of citizens.

After his departure, the tumult continues in the portion of the crowd which remains, scattered on the benches of the Chamber, in the hemicycle, and in the aisles.)

M. Ledru-Rollin. Citizens! you understand that you are committing here a grave act, in naming a provisional government.

Various voices. We don't want it—Yes! yes! we must have one!

M. Ledru-Rollin. In circumstances such as ours, what every citizen must do is to keep silent and to pay attention to the men who want to make up the representatives. . . . (Interruption.) Therefore, listen to me.

We are going to do something serious. There were some demands a little while ago. A provisional government cannot be named in such a light fashion. Do you want to let me read to you the names which seem to be proclaimed by the majority? (Silence!—listen! listen!)

As I read the names, according to whether they are agreeable to you or not, you will shout *yes* or *no* (Very good!—listen!); and, in order to make it official, I beg the stenographers of the *Moniteur* to take note of the names as I pronounce them, because we can't present to France names which have not been approved by you. (Speak! Speak!)

I read:

Dupont (de l'Eure).	(Yes! yes!)
Arago.	(Yes! yes!)
Lamartine.	(Yes! yes!)
Ledru-Rollin.	(Yes! yes!)
Garnier-Pagès.	(Yes! yes!—No!)
Marie.	(Yes! yes!—No!)
Crémieux.	(Yes! yes!) . . .

I ask to add a word. Allow me, gentlemen!

The provisional government which has just been named has great, immense duties to fulfill. The session is going to have to be closed in order to proceed to the center of government and take all necessary measures for stopping the shedding of blood, so that the people's rights may be established.

Numerous cries. Yes! yes! To the City Hall! . . .

A young man. It's not the City Hall that is the center of government. It's here!

(M. Ledru-Rollin retires, followed by several citizens.)

The crowd which had invaded the hall begins to fall off. . . .

A citizen climbs on the marble of the rostrum brandishing a weapon. Someone shouts *Long live the Republic! Let us set out for the City Hall!*

A young man at the rostrum. No more civil list!

Another. No more royalty!

Someone suddenly calls attention to the large picture above the rostrum and behind the president's chair, which represents the taking of the oath to the Charter by Louis Philippe, and cries of *It must be torn up! it must be destroyed!* are immediately heard.

Some men who have climbed onto the rostrum make ready to give saber and sword slashes to the picture.

A worker, armed with a double-barreled gun, who is in the hemicycle, shouts: *Wait! I am going to fire at Louis Philippe!* At the same instant, two shots burst forth. Various cries.

Another worker darts forth immediately to the rostrum, and says:

"Respect for the monuments! respect for property! why destroy? why fire at pictures? We have shown that the people must not be badly led; let us demonstrate now that the people know how to respect monuments and be a credit to its victory!"

These words, pronounced with energy and true eloquence, are drowned out with applause.

They press around the good worker and ask him his name. He says he is named Théodore Six, upholstery worker.

Everyone goes away.

The room is soon completely vacated.

It is past four.

SELECTED BIBLIOGRAPHY

(*See also* footnotes to Readings.)

Aguet, Jean-Pierre, *Contribution à l'étude du mouvement ou-vrier français: les grèves sous la Monarchie de Juillet (1830-1847)*, Genève, 1954.

Allison, John M. S., *Monsieur Thiers*, New York, 1932.

Barzun, Jacques, *Berlioz and the Romantic Century*, 2 vols., Boston, 1949.

Bastide, Paul, *Les Institutions politiques de la monarchie parle-mentaire française (1814-1848)*, Paris, 1954.

Beau de Loménie, E., *Les Responsabilités des dynasties bour-geoises:* Vol. I, *De Bonaparte à Mac-Mahon*, Paris, 1943.

Bertaut, Jules, *Le Roi bourgeois (Louis-Philippe intime)*, Paris, 1937.

Bertier de Sauvigny, G. de, *La Réstauration*, Paris, 1955.

Blanc, Louis, *The History of Ten Years, 1830-1840*, 2 vols., London, 1844-45.

Bruun, Geoffrey, *Revolution and Reaction, 1848-1852* (Anvil Book No. 31), Princeton, 1958.

Cameron, Rondo E., *France and the Economic Development of Europe, 1800-1914*, Princeton, 1961.

Castillon du Perron, M., *Louis-Philippe et la Révolution fran-çaise*, 2 vols., Paris, 1963.

Charléty, S., *La Monarchie de Juillet (1830-1848)*, Paris, 1921.

Chevalier, Louis, *Classes laborieuses et classes dangereuses à Paris pendant la première moitié du XIXe siècle*, Paris, 1958.

Clough, S. B., *France: A History of National Economics*, New York, 1939.

Collins, Irene, *The Government and the Newspaper Press in France*, 1814-1881, London, 1959.

Dansette, Adrien, *Religious History of Modern France*, 2 Vols., New York, 1961.

Dolléans, E., *Histoire du mouvement ouvrier*, Vol. I, 1830-1871, 3rd ed., Paris, 1947.

Dunham, A. L., *The Industrial Revolution in France, 1815-1848*, New York, 1955.

Duroselle, Jean B., *Les Débuts du catholicisme sociale en France, 1822-1870*, Paris, 1951.

Evans, D. O., *Social Romanticism in France, 1830-1848*, New York, 1952.

Guizot, François, *Mémoires pour servir à l'histoire de mon temps*, Paris, 8 vols., 1858-1867.

187

Howarth, T. E. B., *Citizen-King. The Life of Louis Philippe, King of the French,* London, 1961.

Johnson, Douglas, *Guizot: Aspects of French History, 1787-1874,* London and Toronto, 1963.

Kohn, Hans, *Making of the Modern French Mind* (Anvil Book No. 1), Princeton, 1955.

La Gorce, Pierre de, *Louis-Philippe,* Paris, 1931.

Labrousse, Ernest, ed., *Aspects de la crise et de la dépression de l'économie française au milieu du XIXe siècle, 1846-1851,* La Roche-sur-Yon, 1956.

Landes, David, "French Entrepreneurship and Industrial Growth in the Nineteenth Century," *Journal of Economic History,* IX (May, 1949), pp. 45-61.

Ledré, Charles, *La Presse à l'assaut de la monarchie 1815-1848,* Paris, 1960.

Lhomme, Jean, *La Grande bourgeoisie au pouvoir (1830-1880),* Paris, 1960.

Loubère, Leo A., *Louis Blanc, His Life and His Contribution to the Rise of French Jacobin-Socialism,* Chicago, 1961.

Lucas-Dubreton, J., *Louis-Philippe,* Paris, 1938.

————, *The Restoration and the July Monarchy,* New York, 1929.

Manuel, Frank E., *The Prophets of Paris,* Cambridge, Mass., 1962.

Pinkney, David H., "The Crowd in The French Revolution of 1830," *American Historical Review,* LXX (October, 1964), pp. 1-17.

Plamenatz, John, *The Revolutionary Movement in France, 1815-1871,* London, 1952.

Ponteil, F., *La Monarchie parlementaire (1815-1848),* Paris, 1949.

Pouthas, C. H., *La Population française pendant la première moitié du XIXe siècle,* Paris, 1956.

Recouly, Raymond, *Louis Philippe, roi des Français. Le chemin vers le trône,* Paris, 1936.

Rémond, René, *La Droite en France de 1815 à nos jours,* Paris, 1954.

Renouvin, P., *Le XIXe siècle.* I: *De 1815 à 1871* (Vol. V of *Histoire des relations internationales*), Paris, 1954.

Spitzer, Alan B., *The Revolutionary Theories of Louis Auguste Blanqui,* New York, 1957.

Tocqueville, Alexis de, *The Recollections of Alexis de Tocqueville,* ed. by J. P. Mayer, New York, 1949.

Tocqueville, Alexis de, *Oeuvres complètes.* Ed. by J. P. Mayer and others, 9 vols., Paris, 1951 ff.

Vigier, Philippe, *La Monarchie de Juillet,* Paris, 1962.

INDEX

189

VAN NOSTRAND ANVIL BOOKS already published